OLD WORCESTER AS SEEN THROUGH THE CAMERA

FRONT COVER: New Street, view north from junction of Pump Street and Friar Street c1880; the fine Tudor style house dates from about 1600 and is known as Nash House, its name coming from that of Alderman John Nash who lived there during the reign of Charles I. Before Charles Street was made, so as to form the opposite side of the cross roads with Pump Street, the spot was known as Baynham's (or Ballam's) Vine. (JCC/AJB)

BACK COVER: Fully armed Worcester tricyclist in the 1880s: his equipment includes binoculars, bugle, whistle, ink bottle, note pad, quill pen, revolver, two sabres and rifle. (FCE/HC)

OLD WORCESTER
as seen through the camera

BY

CLIVE & MALCOLM HAYNES

BARRACUDA BOOKS LIMITED
BUCKINGHAM, ENGLAND
MCMLXXXVI

PUBLISHED BY BARRACUDA BOOKS LIMITED
BUCKINGHAM, ENGLAND
AND PRINTED BY
BUSIPRINT LIMITED
BUCKINGHAM, ENGLAND

BOUND BY
J.W. BRAITHWAITE & SONS LIMITED
WOLVERHAMPTON, ENGLAND

JACKET PRINTED BY
CHENEY & SONS LIMITED
BANBURY, OXON

PHOTOLITHOGRAPHY BY
CAMERA GRAPHICS LIMITED
AMERSHAM, ENGLAND

TEXT SET IN BASKERVILLE BY
GRAHAM BURN TYPESETTING
LEIGHTON BUZZARD, ENGLAND

ISBN 0 86023 249 2

CONTENTS

ACKNOWLEDGEMENTS

We thank firstly everyone who has made historical material available to us, for without them this book would be very much the poorer, and our knowledge of the past so much less. Space prevents us from reproducing every picture offered, but we do intend them all reaching a wider public.

We are grateful too to all the photographers who so skilfully recorded Worcester's past on glass plate and film, and we have acknowledged the photographer whenever he is known.

Special thanks go to the many Worcester people, fellow local historians and enthusiasts who have assisted us in our researches, in particular Jack Collins, Philip and Helen Curtis, H.W. Gwilliam, Michael Grundy, Pat Hughes, Ann Jenkins, Maurice Jones, Leonard W. Park, David Postle, Ron Shuard, D.G. Trigg and Cora Weaver.

Particular mention must be made of our long suffering friends at the City Museum, Brian Owen and his colleagues, and to Tony Wherry, County Archivist and his staff at Hereford and Worcester County Record Office, County Hall and St Helen's.

Our thanks also go to Gillian Haynes for great assistance in photographic printing, enabling us to gain every subtle nuance from a variety of original pictures, total support, painstaking research and help in preparing the text.

We gratefully acknowledge the valuable publicity created for us by *Worcester Evening News* and *Worcester Source*, thereby bringing our work to a wider public. Thanks are also due to Betty Wilce and Anna Campbell for typing the main body of the work, and to the staff of the County Library Service for their assistance in the subscription arrangements.

KEY TO CREDITS

The photographs in this book, with few exceptions, span the century from 1850 to 1950. Where the photographer is known, his initials appear first, followed by those indicating the source. Where the photographer is unknown, the source only is shown. Sometimes the photographer and the source are one and the same.

AB	A. Barson	DP	David Postle	KB	Ken Beard	RJC	R. Jack Collins
ADMcG	A.D. McGuirk	DRH	Doris R.	K1935	*Kellys Directory*	RPB	R.P. Bryan
AFC	A.F. Clarke		Haynes		1935	RS	Ron Shuard
AG	A. Gray	DT	Douglas Tansell				
AGB	Anthony G.			LG	L. Gould	SAT	S.A. Tarran
	Bethell	ECH	Eric C. Hodson	LT	L. Tonkinson	SD	Sid Draper
ACJ	A.C. Jensen	EFT	E.F. Tipton	LWP	L.W. Park	SN	S. Naish
AJB	A.J. Ballard	EG	Eric Green	L1908	*Littlebury's Street*		
A.J.F-R	Ann and John	EJH	E.J. Homer		*Directory* 1908	TBC	The Ballard
	Fownes-Rigden			L1912	*Littlebury's Street*		Collection
AMB	A.M. Bryan	F	Mr Finch		*Directory* 1912	TBS	T. Bennett &
AN	A. Neal	FCE	F.C. Earl				Sons
AP	Audrey Pearson	FHB	F.H. Brown	MA	Margaret Arney	TW	Terry Wells
AV	Arthur Vale			MHT	M.H. Taylor	TWM	T.W. Marsden
AW	Adrian Wood	GDP	Garston D.	MKC	Marshall Keene		
AWW	A.W. Wright		Phillips		& Co	VS	Violet Simpkins
		GL	George Lewis	MKCA	Marcel K.		
BB	Barclays Bank	GLC	G.L. Copson		Callow	WAW	*Worcester at Work*
BC	Bernard Croad			MO	M. Oakey		1903
BCB	B.C. Brown			MP	Mrs Prior	WC	Worcester
BO'H	Brian	H	Mr Hewlett				Cathedral
	O'Halloran	HAEH	Henry A.E.	N	Mr Neat	WCM	Worcester City
BM	Bishops Move		Haynes	NU	Norwich Union		Museum
B 1855	*Billings Directory*	HC	H. Cooling			WDE	*Worcester Daily*
	1855	HDG	Hazel D. Gorst	PB	Pat Barker		*Echo*
BWJ	*Berrows Worcester*	HWCA	Hereford and	PP	Peggy Pringle	WDT	*Worcester Daily*
	Journal		Worcester	PPS	Percy Parsons		*Times*
CG	Christine Grant		County	PS	Miss P. Shaw	WE	*Worcestershire*
CH	C. Hughes		Archives	PW	P. Waldwyn		*Echo*
CMH	Clive and	JAB	J.A. Brown			WEN	*Worcester Evening*
	Malcolm	JAG	J.A. Goode	RE	R. Elt		*News*
	Haynes	JB	John Bonnett	REJ-R	R. Ellis James-	WHK	W.H. King
		JC	J. Cane		Robertson	WPB	W.P. Briggs
DB	Don Baker	JJC	John J. Cam	RFJ	R.F. Jones	WS	Wally Sutton
DEP	D.E. Phipps	JL	J. Lampitt	RH	Robert Homer	WWH	Walter W.
DG/i	David Glover	JOB	J.O. Brettell	RHGB	Robert Homer-		Harris
DG/ii	Miss D. Glover	JW	J. Webb		'Gipsy Bazaar'		
					1908		

FOREWORD

by Michael Grundy

Graphic insights into our past add an extra dimension to our lives. They give a comforting enrichment by revealing many of the foundations of the social scene and local environment we have inherited.

Undoubtedly the treasury of pictorial evidence captured so richly in the pages of this book will renew electrically for many that insatiable interest in the Worcester of yesteryear. We can stroll down a labyrinth of photographic memory lanes to see again places we may have once known, or which were part of the daily scene for our parents or grandparents.

Through the eyes of professional photographers of old or by family snapshots we can glimpse Worcester people of the last century at work, at play, or simply enjoying the pleasures of their City.

We can see too how Worcester has developed and changed shape and how, alas, it has been knocked-about-a-bit by latter-day Cromwells though, thankfully, it is now enjoying a renaissance.

But, as we look back through the eyes of the camera, we must not be blinkered by the cosy aura of many old photographs, from realising that the times in which they were taken were not always 'The Good Old Days'. Real poverty and deprivation were rife, yet through it all we still seem to sense an atmosphere of true community not readily to be found in the hurly-burly of modern life.

Congratulations go again to Clive and Malcolm Haynes who have done so much since 1967 to bring alive a widespread interest in Worcester's colourful past, through their meticulous researches and their ever-blossoming wealth of photographic archives.

Many thousands have already enjoyed their sophisticated 'Changing Face of Worcester' audio-visual show, and audiences are now according equal acclaim to their second large-scale production, 'Worcester Cathedral in Focus'.

Within this book, Clive and Malcolm lovingly and expansively display our roots, for those of us for whom Worcester is the place of our upbringing or adoption. I feel sure that all those delving into this volume will derive lasting pleasure from the panoramic view of Worcester life it projects, through nearly 300 vintage photographs.

Michael Grundy

INTRODUCTION

In 1964 we became interested in the pictorial history of Worcester. Being keen photographers, we allied our delvings into archives with a commitment to record on film the 'modern' development and progress of the City. 1967 saw the very first presentation of our audio-visual programme 'The Changing Face of Worcester'. The response was enthusiastic. Encouraged by this reaction, we continued our researches and expanded our horizons. Since then the presentation has been many times revised and has embraced several technical improvements. To date, some 25,000 people have seen the show, and many have presented us with historical material, helping to swell our collection of 7,000 slides and prints.

Responding to requests, 1978 saw the publication of our previous book *Yesterday's Town: The Changing Face of Worcester*, produced with the co-authorship of Brian Adlam.

In this book we have not sought to repeat the content of the previous volume. Here, we refer much more to the ordinary folk and 'work-a-day' life and times of the City. We look at the Worcester of our parents and grandparents, to understand something of the texture and fabric of the City that would have been familiar to them.

We hope that everyone will find the scenes and faces of the Worcester of yesteryear as fascinating and absorbing as we do, and that this book will contribute something to the better appreciation of the City which we hold in trust.

Dedication

To our parents, Harry and Doris Haynes
for their early encouragement and enthusiasm,
enduring love of the City and continued support
in the production of our audio-visual
programme and this book.

ABOVE: Worcester Cathedral c1875: notice the Rose Window at the west end, and the Prebendal House, built upon the area of the ancient monastic *rere dorter*; (WC) BELOW: view from south west c1912. The large Prebendal House has now been removed. The steps on the opposite bank were for access to the Cathedral Ferry, just below the Water Gate Lodge of ferryman Giles Wain. (RJC)

THE SHAPE OF THE CITY

Worcester owes its very existence, set upon the banks of the winding river Severn, to the location of an ancient fording place across the waters and the gently sloping river terraces, where travellers could rest and later set up their dwellings. The Romans made it a more permanent settlement, and during Saxon times a group of missionaries sent by Princess Hilda of Whitby established a monastic community. They erected a small church, the very beginnings of the great Cathedral that was to rise during the 12th century. The City grew in importance during succeeding centuries, situated on one of Europe's great trading rivers, and at the only bridging point between Gloucester and Bridgnorth.

First the textile, then the gloving and boot and shoe industries, were the staple trades in and around the bustling market town. Foundries and engineering works followed during the 18th and 19th centuries, as canals and railways connected the City to the 'Black Country'; the manufacture of porcelain was established in the mid–1700s.

An insight into the ancient character of the City can readily be gained by walking around the central area and looking at the street names. Here many trades and professions can be identified. Mealcheapen Street was derived from the sale of meal or corn, while the Cornmarket took its name from the trade in this essential commodity, and was the commercial hub of the City. The Shambles derived from 'flesh shambles', flesh benches for the sale of meat, and was for many years the principal street of butchers. In 1937 there were 17 butchers and a tripe dresser in the street as well as the Butchers Arms pub, now the site of Marks and Spencers. Salt Lane took its name from the route used by salt traders, skirting the City Walls to avoid taxes, as they journeyed to the riverside. Glover Street and Needler Street were so called from the concentration of the gloving industry, while Pierpoint Street owes its name to Matthew Pierpoint, an eminent 19th century surgeon in the City. Orchard Street and Cherry Orchard were the sites of beautiful orchards.

A great number of streets changed their names throughout the years. The following list gives some examples.

Old Street Names

Baker / Baxter Street to Shambles
Bedlam Lane to Thorneloe Road
Bishop Street to Palace Yard (now the south end of Deansway)
Britteport / Birdport (now part of Deansway)
Brodestrete / Broode Street to Broad Street

Castle Grounds to College Street
Church Street to St Peter's Street
Clap Gate to St Martin's Gate
Clements Street to Tybridge Street
Cokenstrete / Cooken Street to Copenhagen Street
Corncheapen to Queen Street
Corviserstrete to Fish Street
Cut Throat Lane to Lansdowne Road

13

Dish Market to Church Street

Eport Street to Newport Street

Forest Street to Foregate Street
Frerenstrete to Friar Street
Frog Lane to Severn Street

Garden Market to St Nicholas Street
Gardeners Lane to Shaw Street
Gloucester Road to Bath Road
Glover Street to New Street
Gosethrote Lane / Goose Throttle or Goose Lane to
St Swithin's Street

Harbour Hill to Tunnel Hill
High Timber Street to Severn Street
Hinton Lane to Hylton Road
Huxterstrete to Little Fish Street (now part of
Deansway)

Incle to Hylton Road

Mary Vale to Merry Vale (now Deansway)
Melechepyng to Mealcheapen Street

Needler Street to Pump Street

Rush Alley to Bridge Street

St Mary's Steps to College Precincts
St Lawrence's Lane to Union Street
Salt Lane to Castle Street
Sansome Fields to Sansome Walk

Todmorden Knol to Edgar Street
Tolley's Hill to Tallow Hill
Town Ditch to Sansome Street
Turkey Street / Torquay Street to Tybridge Street

Union Lane (from the 'Union' or workhouse once on
the Hopmarket site) to St Nicholas Street

Vine Street to Pump Street

Withy Walk to St Paul's Street
Wooden Stair Street to Quay Street

ABOVE: Aerial view of Diglis area c1920: left of the 318ft x 115ft dock, with its swing bridge, is Aston's Timber Yard; the 'basin' area can be seen mid-left hand side. (KB) OPPOSITE ABOVE: Scaffolding above the nave roof — the Victorian restoration of the Cathedral was under way during the 1860s. The west window is pre-restoration. (WC) BELOW: Stallard's Worcester Distillery and bonded vaults, 1860s — the road to the left is Warmstry Slip. (WC)

14

ABOVE: Aerial view of the river and City from the north west c1920, including the expanse of the South Quay with the wide area of Parade Place and Hood Street, the junctions of Copenhagen Street and the now vanished Warmstry Slip. Dent's Glove Factory is on the far right. Between All Saints and St Andrews is Hounds Lane School. The extreme left archway under the bridge is for railway engines from the Butts siding line. (DP) BELOW: Worcester Bridge c1910: the 1847 iron cantilever extensions, to increase the width of the 1781 original, remained until the widening of 1932. (RS)

ABOVE: South Quay: c1890 with the ship *Atalanta*; (KB) BELOW: c1908: industrial and warehouse properties here include, (left of Parade Place) the Worcester Bottling Company, Francis Willey & Co, wool warehouse; right Henry J. Firkins, hop and seed warehouse, and the Severn Iron Warehouse. (AWW)

ABOVE: North Parade and North Quay, c1885: Newport Street is left of centre, and the Old Rectifying House had yet to be built; railway trucks stand on the quayside, along the Butts spur line; (PPS/RS) LEFT: c1910: the Old Rectifying House and the Hop Warehouse of Henry James Firkins, recently constructed. The former took its name from the distillery which occupied part of the building, (rectifying = distilling spirits). (DP) RIGHT: North Parade during a severe flood about 1930. (KB)

ABOVE: Pile driving during the 1880s on the banks of the river at Pitchcroft, to reduce erosion, the old Grandstand in the background. (TBS/WCM) BELOW: North west view of the Cathedral, with old St Michaels Church (foreground); St Michaels in Bedwardine was founded in 826, demolished c1840. (WCM)

19

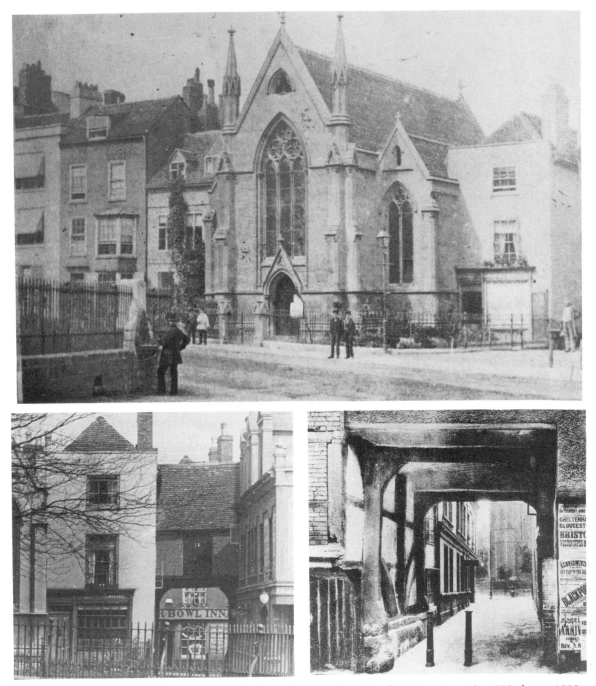

ABOVE: 'New' St Michaels Church was built on the opposite side of College Street in 1839, here c1880, with the drinking fountain set among the Cathedral railings. Closed in 1907, it became the Diocesan Records Office, and was demolished c1962 to make way for the Giffard Hotel complex. (RJC) LEFT: Right of the church was the Lich Gate, connecting College Street to Lich Street; bodies passed through here for burial in the churchyard, north east of the Cathedral. The New Punch Bowl Inn, 15 Lich Street, is through the archway. Right of the gateway was Ye Olde Punch Bowl, 7 College Street. Left of the Lich Gate is 6 College Street, where Henry Handley made violins, from the age of 40. In 1919, in his 80th year, he completed his 100th stringed instrument. (WC) RIGHT: The Lich Gate from Lich Street c1908. (RS)

20

LEFT: Ye Olde Deanery, Lich Street, in 1908: No 32 was occupied by Edward Hawkes, a shoemaker. (RS) RIGHT: Nos 30, 32 and 34 Lich Street, east end; junction with Friar Street to the left and Sidbury to the right. On the corner, McCowen and Co, Leather Merchants. Lich Street was levelled about 1963 for the Giffard Hotel complex. (RS) BELOW: Sidbury, east side, Nos 53 to 41 and a queue during World War I, to Balley Bros Family Grocers Shop (no 53); next door (No 51) was Alfred Hobsons, Hosier and General Outfitters; No 49 contained Mrs J Wilkins, China and Glass Dealer and E. Wilkins & Son, Builders; No 47 was Finch & Co, the Sidbury Button Works, manufacturers of patent solid leather buttons. All have now been demolished and City Walls Road occupies most of the site. (JB)

ABOVE: Sidbury, west side, junction with College Street on left, c1908. In 1908 the list of occupants of the premises reading right to left, using the 'old numbering' is as follows: No 31 (extreme right) Thomas Greenway Chaplin, family grocer; No 32 (white blind) Nathanial Clapton, baker and confectioner; No 33 William Thorneloe Horniblow & Son, family and dispensing chemists; No 34a (arched doorway) Alec Hadley, maltster; No 34 (beneath the Thomas Cook sign) John Frederick Santonna, electrician, dealer in cycles and fireworks, Captain of Worcester Tricycle and Bicycle Club; above is the Midland Railway Parcel Receiving Office; No 35 Sidbury House, Miss L. R. Thorne, draper; next – entrance to Court No 5; No 36 (white front); No 36a Albert Parker, carpenter; No 37 William Birbeck, ironmonger; No 38 Stuart Henshaw Menzies, leather belting manufacturer, and left, on College Street Corner, is 'Ye Caxtons

Head', premises of Evan Humphreys, printer and stationer. (EH) BELOW LEFT: Sidbury, view to the south from the junction with College Street, c1900. At the extreme right is the Victoria Temperance Hotel, (now Inglenooks Tearooms and Restaurant) and the Angel Commercial Hotel, which was the District Office of Mitchells and Butlers Gold Medal Ales & Stouts. This building and properties to the south have all been demolished. However, the entrance to Court No 9 remains today. (RS) BELOW RIGHT: Sidbury, view to the south from Danesbury House (LH side), c1904; note the tram lines, overhead arms for the electric tram wires and elegant 'tear-drop' street lamp. (RS) Sidbury derived from Southbury, or Sudbury and grew up around the Sidbury Gate, the southern access to the City.

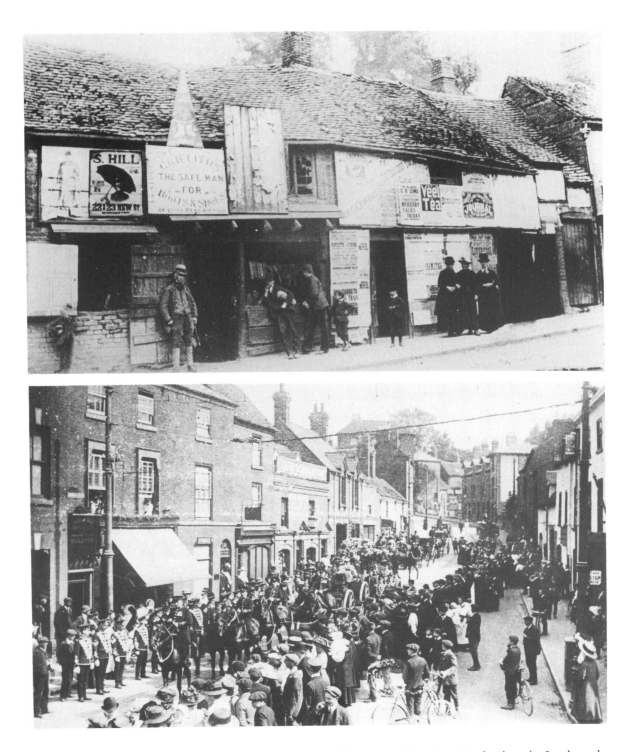

ABOVE: London Road, c1850, possibly in the area of the Cross Keys Inn. Destinations in Leeds and Liverpool are advertised on some of the posters and people seem to be waiting. (HDG) BELOW: Military funeral c1915 at the bottom of London Road, near the junction with Bath Road: the coffin is on a gun carriage and a coach is just leaving the shoeing smiths of G. V. Johns, next door to the Cross Keys Inn; left is the office of local builders Bromage and Evans.

LEFT: Wylds Lane c1926, from east of the junction with Albert Road; the Post Office was at No 232, Postmistress Mrs Rogers, and the office was only open for 18 months before moving to the Derby Road corner of Wylds Lane. The Lane took its name from the Wyld family who lived at the Commandery at the Sidbury end in the19th century. (DB) BELOW: Sidbury and St Peters Church, Kings Street area — view from the north c1930. The Parish of St Peters was a mass of small houses and courts; RIGHT: the street directory of 1908 gives us an insight into the character of St Peters Street and Kings Street. (CMH)

25

LEFT: St Peters Street, south side at junction with Sidbury c1920; (EFT) CENTRE: St Peters Church (N); RIGHT: St Peters Street, north side c1920. (EFT) St Peters Street was previously Church Street. Saint Peter the Great (known as 'The Great' to differentiate between it and Saint Peter the Little, a chapel at the Castle – near where the Kings School is today) replaced a previous church which only held 275. 'New' St Peters became redundant when most of its parish was demolished, the cottages on the right being levelled in June 1950, the Tudor-style house on the left some ten years later and the church itself reduced in 1971. BELOW: View from St Andrews Church spire toward Birdport junction with Powick Lane, c1925; the City Rag Stores of William Prosser occupied 22 to 28, established 1860. The building between the Rag Stores and the entrance to Countess of Huntingdon's Church was once Edward Beesley, fried fish shop and P. J. Walley's grocery store, (1908). (TWM/WCM)

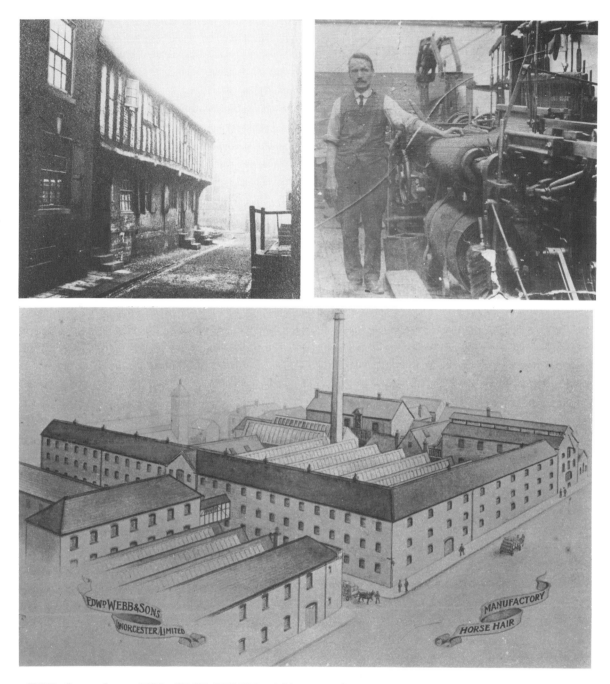

LEFT: Group Lane c1900. (CMH) BELOW: Webb's Horsehair Carpet Factory was in Birdport between Bull Entry and Copenhagen Street. At 27 years, Edward Webb established it in 1835 at 8 Copenhagen Street. Webbs horse-hair carpet foot rugs were used by most of the early railway companies in Britain. In later years, the firm supplied carpets for Prime Minister Gladstone at 10 Downing Street in 1892, and 600 yards of carpet for a processional way at the wedding of the Duke of York, later George V, and for his coronation in 1910. In 1935 the factory moved to Sherriff Street and the Police Station was built on the Deansway site. Edward Webb founded the only factory school in Worcester. He became Mayor 1847–8 and played a prominent role in City life. (JW) RIGHT: Walter Woodward making the carpet for the coronation of George V. (PS)

LEFT: Members of Edward Webb's staff on the factory roof at Birdport; St Andrews spire is in the background. Mr Edward Webb, founder, is holding the book, 7 September 1926. (F) BELOW: West from St Andrews Church c1935. At the extreme left is Warmstry Slip where a horse and cart are just leaving the yard of the Severn Valley Pickle Company, and rowing boats are moored. Further right is South Quay and Copenhagen Street, and centre is a view into Court No 6 cottages and houses in Quay Street area. Hound's Lane School is at the right hand side. (ADMcG/WCM)

RIGHT: Court No 6 with a lady washing the steps of her home, a pair of socks on a line, and a dog and cat in the sunshine.

LEFT: The junction of Copenhagen Street and Birdport, c1936, and the demolition of No 18, the Corner House, and home of Mrs 'Titty' Brace. St Andrews Church was originally built in the 12th century. The spire was added to the 15th century tower in 1751 by Nathaniel Wilkinson. (WEN/WCM) RIGHT: Copenhagen Street, view from west after clearance, 1947. Model Dwellings in background, an early 'council' development, built 1855, demolished 1955. (HWCA) BELOW: South side of Copenhagen Street c1931 showing a house that at one time had a magnificent and ornate barge board. It was previously called Cucken ('Cooking' or 'Cucking'/'Ducking'), Street, and renamed Copenhagen Street to commemorate Nelson's famous victory of 1801. (ADMcG/WCM)

30

ABOVE: Copenhagen Street, junction with South Quay c1930, and St Andrews' Institute, formerly the Wherry Inn, with its maze of cellars. Many South Quay cellars reached well towards the High Street. The general stores next door belonged to William Jeynes; Mrs Jeynes cut hair for ladies and children. The son, Bill Jeynes, owned the well known hardware warehouse in Tybridge Street which closed in 1985. (WCM) BELOW: Copenhagen Street c1931. The archway just beyond the car is the entrance to The Bridewell, an early form of workhouse in use between 1614 and the early 18th century, when the 'House of Industry', (latterly known as Hillborough) was opened at Tallow Hill. (ADMcG/WCM)

ABOVE: Broad Street, c1900: right of centre is the Bell Hotel, a coaching inn. The proprietor was Thomas Stanley D'Aeth. The hotel and properties behind it along Little Angel Street, (the entrance to which can be seen between the hotel and Dingle, Son & Edwards) were demolished in 1913 to create Angel Place. (WWH/HWCA) BELOW: Broad Street, c1906: the Crown Hotel, right; another City coaching inn, with its ornate balcony and William IV (c1830) lamps, well remembered for its Glee Room and 'Men Only' room. Before Worcester was connected to London by railway, tickets were purchased just inside the entrance for the Spetchley Railway Station horse omnibus. Further down the street, past Blackfords drapers at No 11, two large eyes advertise optician Render Layfield at No 14. (RS)

ABOVE: Angel Place and Five Ways c1855, looking across the Sheepmarket to the alley leading to the 1859 Congregational Church; right, Worcester Homoeopathic Dispensary, once the minister's house and right again, the Phoenix Fire Engine House, later Norwich Union; left, the vestry and above, Worcester's first public subscription library and further left, Lewis Clarke's Brewery. (WCM) BELOW: Dolday, view from the west, c1931: the children are by Court No 3, which led to Wellington Square. The All Saints Workhouse was the next building up on the left. On the distant bend is the Sow and Pigs Inn and at the 'end', the four windowed house is the Woolpack Inn. (ADMcG/WCM)

ABOVE: Dolday c1930; looking west, showing the north side with Court 3. The building in the foreground was once All Saints Workhouse. The Watermans Church is in the distance. (ADMcA/WCM)
LEFT: The corner of Shaw Street and Five Ways c1900: Fishers old corner shop, a hairdresser's premises during the early 1900s, it stood adjacent to the Five Ways Inn, licensee Thomas Hopwood. (WCM)
RIGHT: Angel Street, view to the east c1880: the fine lamps on the left are along the frontage of the Theatre Royal, opposite the Fountain Inn. (JC/AJB)

ABOVE: The Cross c1908 from the junction with Broad Street: left is the tailor's shop of R. A. Roberts & Co, and beyond, John Richard Parsons Hosiery shop and Salmon and Gluckstein, tobacconists. The imposing frontage of Lloyds Bank, built in 1861, is opposite. In the centre, at the corner of St Nicholas Street is the Public Benefit Boot Company (Lennards Ltd). (RS) BELOW: The Cross, view to south from junction with St Nicholas Street c1896: the semi-circular steps are outside St Nicholas Church, and the impressive pilastered frontage midway along the right hand side was, until about 1920, the shop of J. Turley & Co (No 27) General Drapers, silk merchants and carpet warehousemen. (RS)

ABOVE: Aerial view of St Nicholas Church and St Martins Church area from the west c1920: tramlines are visible in St Nicholas Street with W. R. Higgs Glass Merchants just behind St Nicholas Church (built c1735); behind St Martins Church (built in 1772) is the west elevation of the Public Hall; left, St Martins School and playground, established 1836 by voluntary subscriptions. (RS) LEFT: Queen Elizabeth House c1880. Elizabeth I addressed the citizens of Worcester in 1575 from the balcony of this house. When it was decided to extend Trinity Street through to St Nicholas Street, it stood directly in the way, and was in danger of demolition. Instead, it was moved across the road in 1891 by jacking it up and sliding it on greased railway lines the 30 or so feet involved. The Derby Road company of Bromage & Evans undertook the work. It is still there today. (JC/AJB) RIGHT: Moving the house in 1891. (RS)

ABOVE: Cornmarket was for centuries the open air trading centre of Worcester: stalls, stocks and pillory, and at one time gallows, upon which severed limbs were displayed, were here. When it was decided to build a corn market, political rivalry generated the Corn Exchange in Angel Street in 1849, ousting its rival in the Cornmarket, which was used as a Music and Public Hall. Here Charles Dickens gave readings, Souza played, Jenny Lind sang and both Elgar and Dvorak conducted. It became a British Restaurant during World War II, a bingo hall, 'The Majestic' in the 1960s, and was demolished in 1966 to provide a car park. The Public Hall c1880, left; the Plough Inn centre, and the then narrow entrance to St Martins Gate, also known as Clap Gate, from the gate in the City Wall. (JJC/AJB) BELOW: The pawnbroker's shop of Joseph Coleman c1910, is left of centre, with Brown's drapery store on the right. (DG/i)

ABOVE: Mealcheapen Street c1903, from Cornmarket: the public house (right) is the Royal Exchange Vaults; a noted restaurant was The Shades which, under the management of Mrs Ada Yarnold, speciailised in tripe. (RS) LEFT: The Shambles to the north c1880, showing west side; the Butchers Arms is on the left and RIGHT: the east side, with the long barber's pole at No 38. John Cam took both these photographs, and was the son of W. H. Cam, who had a business in the Shambles at No 32, where he manufactured glovers' knives, sewing machines and presses. (Both JC/AJB)

ABOVE: New Street, east side, northern end, c1900; Nos 22 and 23 were occupied by Samuel Hill & Sons, trunk and umbrella manufacturers, beyond which is the Old Pheasant Inn of 1580, so called when Mrs Eleanor Morris, a widow, bought it in 1787, having previously kept an inn of the same name in Silver Street. It was much frequented for bowling and the scene of many cock fights. (EFT) BELOW: New Street, to the north, with Nash House, c1900: the 'books' are above the Steam Printing and Bookbinding Works of Baylis, Lewis & Co, and to its right is Masters, dispensing chemists, 'Maker of the Celebrated Cough Pills'. (RS)

ABOVE: Friar Street, west side from the south c1912; the black and white Tudor Coffee House, now Tudor House Museum, was built in the early 1500s; in 1615 Harry Wheeler, a weaver, lived there with servants. (RS) BELOW: In 1908 Nos 34 to 40 included, extreme left, the shop of John Sigley & Son, manufacturing confectioners. (RS)

ABOVE: Greyfriars and Friar Street c1900: for many years Greyfriars was believed part of the Fransciscan Friary buildings, which occupied an extensive area where Lasletts Alsmhouses now stand. However, recent research indicates that Greyfriars was first built in the 1400s for Thomas Green, a brewer and innkeeper. Later the entrance led to Georges Yard, a court with ten dwellings named after the family who occupied part of Greyfriars from about 1724 to 1841. Greatly restored by Mr Matley Moore and his sister Elsie, the National Trust now owns the building. (H) BELOW: Friar Street with right, The Eagle Vaults c1910, and the hardware shop of Edward J. Goodwin on the left. (RS)

LEFT:The Wesleyan Methodist Church in Pump Street (in 1940), was originally an Independent chapel taken over in 1795, subsequently demolished, and a larger one built in 1813, again to be demolished and re-built in 1837. It stood until 1965, to be replaced by the present church, opened in 1966. Pump Street was previously called Needler Street and Vine Street. (RS) BELOW: Foregate Street and The Foregate, aerial view from the north c1920: right is the cleared area of Angel Place before the construction of the Scala Cinema. The Sheep Market area is being covered over for the Worcester Fruit and Vegetable Market, and right of this is the Congregational Church. (WCM) RIGHT: The Foregate from the railway bridge c1880, with the Hopmarket Commercial Hotel, which was re-built in the late Victorian/Edwardian terra-cotta style. (DG/i)

ABOVE: The Star Hotel in the Foregate, c1912. The high sides to the railway bridge were constructed to prevent the steam engines frightening horses. Originally the Star and Garter, it was one of the principal coaching inns of the City, with one of the most widely used cock-fighting pits in the county. Established about 1588, the Star was the top hotel from 1780 to 1840, and again under the management of George Edwin Spurr from 1908 to 1930. (EFT) BELOW: Foregate Street from junction on right with Pierpoint Street, looking north c1950: the Post Office occupied Nos 17 and 18 (once a bank and the house of Dr Pierpoint), and opened here in 1868 — until the new Post Office was built at 8 Foregate Street in 1953. (AWW)

ABOVE: The Tything, north from the junction with St Mary's Street c1930: the Saracens Head Inn, in the 19th century had a fashionable bowling green, and to the right was Tything House, a private hotel. Premises on the left included F. W. Coomber & Son, radio engineers, J. P. Foy, photographers and William Austin, piano dealer. The name probably derived from the early English 'Tithing', a district containing ten householders. (RS) BELOW: Shewrings Alms Houses, The Tything, c1912, were founded by Thomas Shewring, Mayor in 1682 and 1687, for six poor women from different parishes. In 1912 the charity was administered by 'The Six Masters' and the six widows resident received nine shillings a week; right is McNaughts garage, and the site is today occupied by Kay & Co Ltd, Tything Offices. (EJH/RH)

LEFT: Barbourne Lodge, after being deliberately set on fire in March 1906; it stood to the south of Barbourne Brook at the junction of Barbourne Lane and Waterworks Road, and in its time was a Bedlam (lunatic asylum) in the early 1700s, the private residence of Richard Burnley (1760s) where he ran a school for music and dance and, towards the end of the 19th century, a fever hospital. It was burned down to destroy any trace of infection, then demolished. (HWCA) BELOW: Lindisfarne House and its extensive ornamental gardens, in Barbourne Terrace in 1910. George Gascoyne senior bought the house in 1909 — the Gascoynes were hop and seed merchants in Sansome Street. He died in 1931 aged 65, and his widow in 1950 at the age of 91. The house was them sold to Dr Crowe, but is now occupied by the National Farmers Union, the gardens having been largely built over. (PP) RIGHT: George Gascoyne with his daughter at Lindisfarne c1911: the car is probably a Humber. (PP)

ABOVE: A garden party at Lindisfarne House in 1911, for members of the Shakespeare Society. (PP) BELOW: Near the north end of Pitchcroft, once stood the Water Tower, part of the 18th century Waterworks, here c1915. Water was pumped from the nearby Severn to a tank at the top of the tower, and thence to the central reservoir, then in the Trinity near Queen Elizabeth's House. It supplied water until 1858 and stood until the 1950s. (WCM)

ABOVE: The Norman Church of St John assumed its role as Parish Church in 1371; the graveyard was cleared in the 1960s. (WCM) LEFT: The weighbridge in St John's c1908; the grocer and provision merchant's shop is that of Robert Birch, who was also the collector for the weighbridge. (WCM) RIGHT: Rooming house c1890, next to Powells Row, St John's, and now Barclays Bank. (BB)

ABOVE: Comer Road, St John's, looking north from the junction with Lambert Road, c1915: Henry Ford Griffith's bakery is next door to the Brewers Arms, licensee Fred Short. (RS) BELOW: Henwick Road, St John's: the east side, probably Nos 36 to 50, c1900: in 1908 a tin worker, china worker, journeyman leather dresser, journeyman brushmaker and railway plate layer lived here. (RS)

ABOVE: The area between Bromwich Lane and New Road, awaiting the making of Bromwich Road, looking north; in the distance, Cripplegate House, c1928. (EJH/RH) BELOW: Bromwich Lane and cottages at junction with Swanpool Walk. (RS)

ABOVE: St John's Infants Class II, c1896, Ethel Horton, wearing a dark dress, sixth from left second row; teacher (top left) is Martha Horton, daughter of Sam Horton, blacksmith, St John's, later Post Mistress at St John's Post Office. (SAT) BELOW: St Stephen's School staff 1899 with Mesdames Marks, Cropper, Martin, Barker, Rofe, Whittall, Diaper, Whitehouse, Pierce and Gegg. (DG/ii)

FROM SCHOOL TO WORK

Without doubt the oldest school in Worcester is the King's School, founded by Henry VIII in 1541, and following the dissolution of the monastery attached to the Cathedral. The Royal Grammar School, too, has claims to antiquity, with its Elizabethan charter dating from 1561. Schools for the 'ordinary folk' of Worcester were not established on a regular basis until the beginning of the 19th century. Of fundamental importance was the Lancastrian Monitorial School in St Martin's Gate, established for 'the children of the labouring poor'. Following this example, several other schools were founded, many with church and parish associations.

Finance was always difficult in those early days, and at one low point pupils at the British School had to pay for their lessons in school 'pence'. The range of educational topics offered may appear limited by today's standards, but it gave the pupils an excellent grounding in the 'three R's', preparing them as well as possible for the life of work ahead.

Throughout the centuries Worcester has been synonymous with a wide range of industry. Records of 1173 refer to the cloth industry and the trade of dyeing. Since then the City has seen the rise and decline of other industries, the varying fortunes of gloving, the coming of printing and the increasing importance of the manufacture of porcelain. The development of Worcestershire Sauce and the Vinegar Works of Hill, Evans followed in the 19th century. Engineering companies such as Hardy and Padmore, McKenzie and Holland, Heenan and Froude, Wards, Metal Box, Meco and Archdales produced lamp posts, railway signalling equipment, machine tools, tinware, mining equipment and many other products.

The fluctuating fortunes of the glove industry were of particular importance to Worcester, during the 19th century, as it was the only City in the Kingdom so wholly dependent upon one commodity. In 1834, when 30,000 people in and around Worcester were engaged in glove manufacture, the fickleness of fashion could have a disastrous effect. With over 100 manufacturers in the 1830s, the number had declined by 75% twenty years later. Well known gloving names were those of Fownes, Dent Allcroft, Frank Bryan, Guise and Miloré. The glove-making process was both skilled and arduous. Early processes including 'treading' the cured skins by two men standing in a large barrel with a mixture of good fresh eggs, water and salt. Fownes used duck eggs principally – some 16,000 each week. The 'treading' went on for 14 hours in hot and smelly conditions, all for 9 pence per man. The skins were staked by stretching them over a large semi-circular blunt knife atop a large stake. This process made the skin supple and delicate, bringing up the grain. The skins were next 'pared', in old times using the circular glovers' 'paring knife', later replaced by emery-coated wheels. The cutter skilfully cut the elastic skins into rectangles. The glove pieces or 'tranks' were then cut to shape by punches for the final process of stitching. Frank Bryan's factory, established at Worcester in 1911, specialised in sports gloves. Moving from the Bull Ring to the Bromyard Road factory in 1920, they produced 1,750 flying helmets and electrically heated gauntlets each week for the RAF during the Second World War.

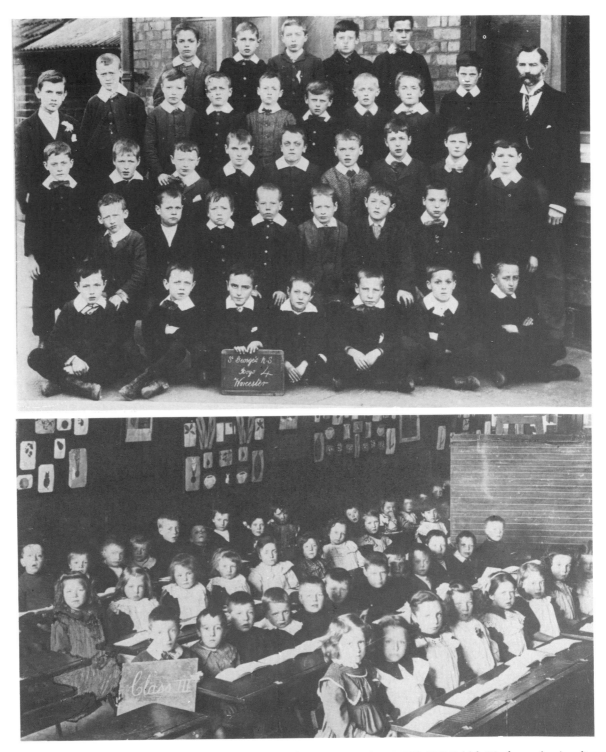

ABOVE: St George's School, St George's Lane, boys, class 4, c1910. (CMH) BELOW: British (Undenominational) School, St Martins Gate/Bowling Green Terrace boys and girls, class III — Violet Griffiths is fourth on the right. (VS)

ABOVE: St Martin's Boys School c1908: Class VI, with headmaster Samuel Riley and his brother Charles 'Bear' Riley, who by 1912 had succeeded as headmaster. (DG/i) BELOW: British School Girls, Group IV: the girl in white three rows back on the left, nearest the centre aisle, is Violet Griffiths. (VS)

ABOVE: The Kings School, c1928, was founded by Henry VIII in 1541; (WCM) BELOW: the Art Room.
(MKC/HWCA)

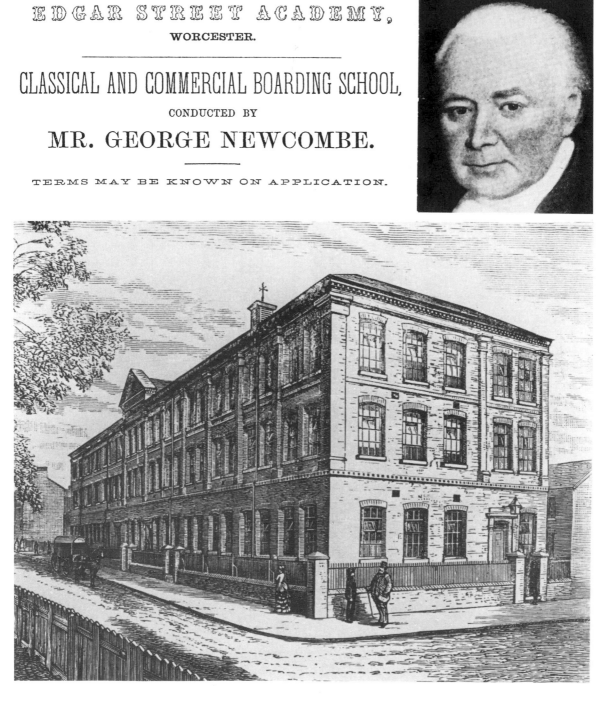

EDGAR STREET ACADEMY,
WORCESTER.

CLASSICAL AND COMMERCIAL BOARDING SCHOOL,

CONDUCTED BY

MR. GEORGE NEWCOMBE.

TERMS MAY BE KNOWN ON APPLICATION.

LEFT: The private sector in 1855. (B1855) RIGHT: Mr John Fownes, founder of Fownes Gloves in 1777. (AJF-R)
BELOW: Fownes factory: an engraving of the 19th century. (AJF-R)

LEFT: Treading the skins in a tub: 19th century method; RIGHT: washing and dyeing the skins by machinery, c1906, (Both AJF-R) and the Dyeing Shop at Fownes c1900. (WCM) Similarly, hand staking the skins was the 19th century method, and 'staking' in 1906 was by machine.

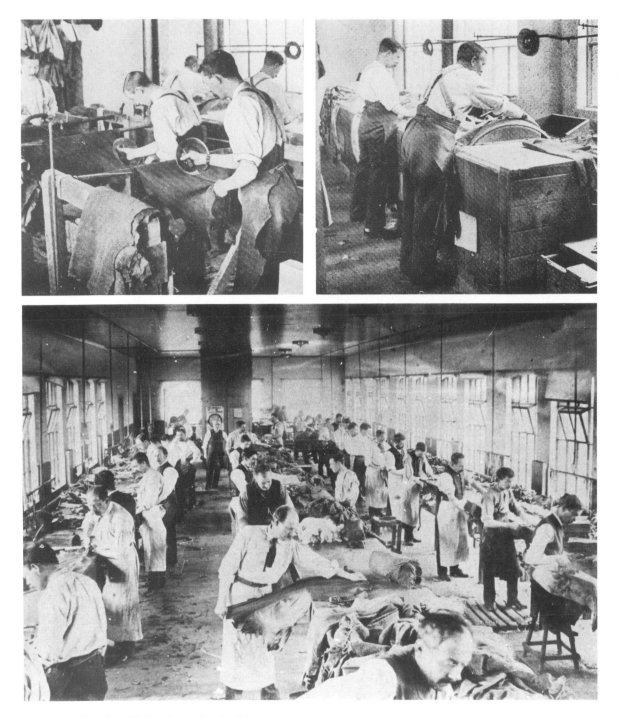

LEFT: Using the old circular paring knife was replaced RIGHT: in 1906 by machines. (Both AJF-R) BELOW: The cutting shops at Fownes c1900 were certainly labour intensive, with some 35 men at work. (WCM)

ABOVE: Glove making by hand, at an outworker's cottage — typical 19th century scene. BELOW: In the 1890s, the Machine Room at Fownes employed almost 100 girls. (Both AJF-R)

ABOVE: A group of managers at Fownes Gloves c1890. (WCM) BELOW: The leather sorting and stock room at Frank Bryans Glove Factory during the early 1930s. (AMB)

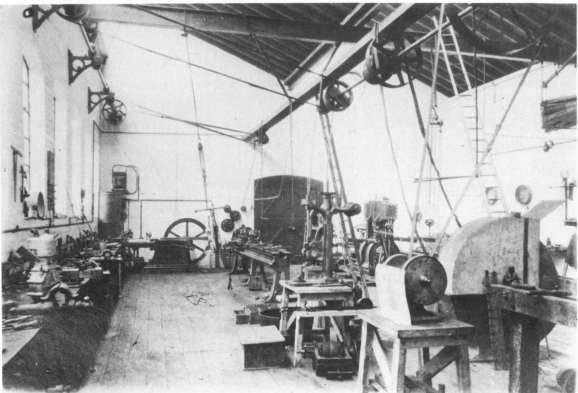

LEFT: Daniel Redler and Co Ltd, City Flour Mills, were established in 1898 when they took over from Weaver & Co. They were well known for their brands of flour 'Eclipse', 'Extras' and 'Pride of the Midlands'. A bran was also made called 'Broad Leaf' which was used as feed for hunting and race horses. They were in Padmore Street, near the canal. Power was derived from a 250 horse power engine. (WAW) BELOW: John J. Cam's workshop in Charles Street, c1890. Having learnt his craft at his father's engineering business (W. Cam) at 32 The Shambles, where they were established in 1850, John Cam set up his own business at the turn of the century. He was a remarkable and inventive engineer. In the 700 square yards of 'works' he produced powerful hydraulic engines for organ blowing at the Cathedral and Public Hall, even exporting one model to Australia. He also produced a 1½ hp tandem and an improved braking system for motor 'cycles. He was a member of the Worcester Tricycle Club and an enthusiastic early photographer. (JJC/AJB) RIGHT: In The Shambles. (B1855)

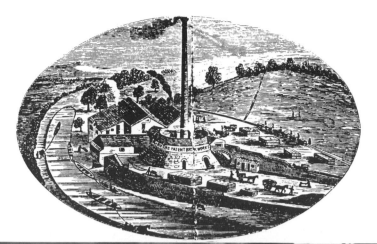

ABOVE: D. W. Barkers Brick Works, 1918: the Worcester Patent Brickworks faced the City Football Ground alongside the canal. (AW) CENTRE: Metal Castings Factory at Droitwich Road c1925, established in Worcester in 1919 with manufacture commencing the following year. Initially the company produced icecream freezing cabinets, motor car sumps and brake shoes. In later years, production included automatic transmissions, parts for Ariel and BSA motor cycles and Servis washing machines. This picture shows melting furnaces for the 'Gravity Casting' process. (RPB) BELOW: Construction of H. W. Ward's factory c1934/35, showing 'first section' viewed from Bilford Road railway bridge. (WS)

ABOVE: Group of Power Station workers outside the Sports and Social Club which they built c1938. Front row (l to r): A. F. Clarke, A. George (joiner), Mr Lee; middle row (l to r): on first step, E. Harrison, W. Floyd (blacksmith), L. Mann, Bill Jukes, unknown, T. Chance; back row (l to r): H. Owen, A. Pugh, E. Harrison Junior, J. Smith, Mr Clarke, Kendel-Smith, S. Pollard (fitter), S. Webb (blacksmith's striker), A. Brian. (SD/AFC)
BELOW: Construction of the new Power Station (Electricity Works); view from North Quay c1942, with part of the old station still visible. (MHT)

ABOVE: The 'Fire King' with crew outside the Norwich Union Fire Office, Five Ways, about 1910. The Worcester office took delivery of the appliance in 1905; it was a 400 gallon per minute, self-propelled steam fire engine, purchased from Merryweather & Sons. An extract from The Brigade's Report Book of 29 July 1905 reads 'Rushwick Manor, new motor fire engine. Farm buildings, ten tons of hay saved. Water from River Teme, ¾ mile distant. New motor engine worked most satisfactorially, engaged 20 hours. 170 gallons oil used.' (This was to fire the boiler – not to keep the fire going! ED.) (NU/TW) BELOW: Cadbury Brothers' Fire Brigade at the Blackpole Factory c1920. (HWCA)

LEFT: Winwood advertise in 1912. (L1912) BELOW: A road accident, but nothing was damaged! A tribute to skilful packing by W. Winwood, established in 1840, whose head office was at 38 The Tything; (BM) ABOVE: The relish that carried the county's name worldwide. (RHGB) CENTRE: In 1855 Richard Dayus sought continuing custom for his fuel and forage business. (B1855)

64

ABOVE: Members of the Tustin family; John Tustin established a 'horse breaking' business at No 4 The Butts c1930. BELOW: Haymaking at Grove Farm c1932. (SAT)

ABOVE: Horse sale at the Cattle Market, The Butts. (BCB) BELOW: Irish store cattle crossing the bridge, heading for the market in the Butts (c1946). (AWW)

DRINKING AND PICKING

At the turn of the century there were around 200 inns, hotels and beer retailers in the City. Their premises ranged from front rooms of terraced houses, with a few barrels set up, to large, purpose-built taverns. Many were ancient coaching inns such as the Bell, Crown, the Star and Garter and the Unicorn. From such places many carriers made their living. In 1908, carriers went out to 123 destinations from some 24 inns within the City. The Old Greyhound was particularly busy on Saturdays, with 19 different carriers leaving for some 50 destinations. Public house names make a fascinating study. Sometimes the derivation is obvious, like the Shakespeare, which was adjacent to the Theatre Royal, or the Ewe and Lamb and the Sow and Pigs, which were close by the Cattle Market. But why Peep o' Day, Bird-in-Hand and Lame Dog? The Old Chapel is a curious one, and so named because it was on the site of a Wesleyan Chapel in New Street.

These are a few examples and, drawing upon six street directories, spanning a century from 1855 to 1955, a fascinating, though not exhaustive list emerges.

As the City was at the centre of a great hop-producing county, it is not surprising that it had seven major breweries, and several pubs which brewed their own beer at the beginning of the 1900s. In the 18th century, Worcester boasted the largest hop market in the country. Established in 1731, it occupied the old Parish Workhouse buildings opposite Berkeley Alms Houses. Annual sales averaged 20,000 'pockets'. Re-development of the Foregate during the 1890s resulted in a new Hop Market and Hotel being built in a decorative, if somewhat flamboyant style.

Worcester's Inns, Taverns and Alehouses

Albert Inn	Belmont Street	Black Horse	Lowesmoor
Albion	Bath Road	Black Lion	Dent Street
Alma	Mill Street	Boars Head	Newport Street
Alma	Droitwich Road	Boat	Lowesmoor
Alma	Lowesmoor	Brewers Arms	Comer Road
Anchor	Diglis Road	Brewers Arms	Moor Street
Angel	St Johns	Bricklayers Arms	Park Street
Angel Hotel	Sidbury	Bridge	Bridge Street
Angel	Silver Street	Bridge	Lowesmoor Terrace
Apple Tree	Tybridge Street	Brunswick Arms	Malvern Road
Arboretum	Northfield Street	Bulls Head	High Street
Arcadia	Broad Street	Bush	Bull Ring
Barbourne Inn	New Bank Street	Butchers Arms	Shambles
Barley Mow	Sidbury	Carpenters Arms	Spring Gardens
Bear	Tybridge Street	Chequers	Hylton Road
Beauchamp Hotel	Broad Street	Chestnut Tree	Lansdowne Road
Bee Hive	Tallow Hill	City Arms	Church Street
Bell	St Johns	Coach and Horses	Upper Tything
Bell	Droitwich Road	Coach and Horses	Shambles
Bell Hotel	Broad Street	Cock	Copenhagen Street
Berkeley Arms	School Road	Cock	Tybridge Street
Berkeley Arms	Bank Street	Commercial Inn	Silver Street
Berwick Arms	Bath Road	Coventry Arms (Cardinals Hat)	Friar Street
Bird in Hand	The Cross	Croft	James Street
Black Boy	Lich Street	Cross Keys	Friar Street

67

Cross Keys	London Road	Horse and Jockey	Pump Street
Crowle House	Hill Street	Imperial Hotel	St Nicholas Street
Crown	Bransford Road	Ketch	Bath Road
— Crown Hotel	Broad Street	King's Head	Sidbury
Crown	Friar Street	King's Head	St Johns
Crown	Tallow Hill	King Williams Vaults	St Pauls Street
Crown and Anchor	Silver Street /	Lamb and Flag	Tything
	Lowesmoor	Lame Dog	Canal Side, Nr Dent
Crown and Anchor	Hylton Road		Street
Diglis House Hotel	Portland Street	Lamp Tavern	Tybridge Street
Dog and Duck	St Nicholas Street	Lansdowne Hotel	Lowesmoor
Dolphin	Copenhagen Street	Lansdowne	Lansdowne Street
Duke of York	Angel Place	— Leopard	Broad Street
Duke of York	Lich Street	Liverpool Vaults	The Shambles
Duke of Wellington	Birdport	Locomotive	George Street
Eagle Vaults	Friar Street	Masons Arms	High Timber Street
Eagle	Pheasant Street		(Severn Street)
Elephant and Castle	Lowesmoor Wharf	Mitre	Lich Street
Ewe and Lamb Vaults	Angel Street	Moors Ketch	The Moors
Ewe and Lamb	The Butts	Mount Pleasant	London Road
Express	Lowesmoor	Mouth of the Nile	Copenhagen Street
— Falcon	Broad Street	Mug House	Hylton Road
Farmers Arms	Little Butts	Navigation	Lowesmoor
Farriers Arms	Farrier Street	Nelson	All Hallows
Farriers Arms	Fish Street	New Inn	George Street
Fish	Diglis Street	New Inn	Ombersley Road
Five Ways	Angel Place	New Inn	The Shambles
Fleece	Mealcheapen Street	New Chequers	Astwood Road
Foresters Arms	Sansome Walk	New Greyhound	New Street
Fort Royal (The Clock)	London Road	New Pope Iron	Pope Iron Road
Fountain	Angel Street	New Punch Bowl	Lich Street
Fountain (Potters	Severn Street	Northwick Arms	Vine Street
Wheel)		Odd Fellows Arms	Carden Street
Four Ways Inn	Charles Street	Old Chappelle	New Street
Fox Inn	Pitmaston Road	Old Crown	Friar Street
Freemasons Arms	Carden Street	Old Crown	Pump Street
(Masons)		Old England	Providence Street
Gardeners Arms	Bransford Road	Old Falcon	Sansome Street
Gardeners Arms	Oldbury Road	Old Farriers	Quay Street
Garibaldi	Bromyard Road	Old Greyhound	New Street
Garibaldi	Wylds Lane	Old Peacock	Queen Street
George and Dragon	Tything	Old Pheasant	New Street
Globe	Friar Street	Old Porter Stores	Copenhagen Street
Glo'ster Arms	Copenhagen Street	Old Rectifying House	North Parade
Glovers Arms	Powick Lane	Old Red Lion	Newport Street
Golden Hart	Sansome Street	Old Severn Trow	Quay Street
Golden Lion	High Street	Pack Horse	St Nicholas Street
Goodrest	Barker Street	Park Tavern	Upper Park Street
Grandstand	Pitchcroft	Park Street Tavern	Little Park Street
Great Western Hotel	Shrub Hill	Paul Pry	The Butts
Green Dragon	Newport Street	Peep o' Day	Cumberland Street
Green Dragon	Tything	Perdiswell House	Droitwich Road
Green Man	Tything	Plough	Fish Street
Grosvenor Arms	Henwick Road	Plough	Silver Street
Gun Tavern	Newtown Road	Plumbers Arms	Wylds Lane
Hare and Hounds	College Street	Plume of Feathers	Tything
Herefordshire House	Bransford Road	Portobello	Bransford Road
Herefordshire House	Newport Street	Potters Arms	St Pauls Street
Hole in the Wall	Merryvale	Press	All Hallows
Holly Bush	St Nicholas Street	Prince of Wales	Shrub Hill Road
Hop Market Hotel	Foregate	Punch Bowl	College Street
Hope and Anchor / Severn	Newport Street	Queen's Arms	Powick Lane
View		Queen Caroline	Quay Street
Horn and Trumpet	Angel Street	Queen's Head	Tything
Horn and Trumpet	Charles Street	Railway Arms	Shrub Hill Road

Railway Bell	St Martins Gate	Swan	Barbourne
Ram	Shrub Hill Road	Swan with Two Nicks	New Street
Raven	Droitwich Road	Talbot	Barbourne Road
Red Lion	Sidbury	Talbot	College Street
Reindeer Hotel	Mealcheapen Street	Talbot	Paradise Row
Rising Sun	Bank Street	Telegraph	George Street
Rising Sun	Clement Street (Tybridge Street)	Ten Bells	Dolday
Rose and Crown	Severn Terrace	Three Tuns	Castle Street
Royal Exchange Vaults	Corn Market	Turks Head	Lowesmoor
Royal George	Hylton Road	Unicorn	Broad Street
Royal Oak	Carden Street	Union	Lowesmoor
Royal Oak	York Place	Union	Union Street
St George's Tavern	St George's Lane	Vaults	Corn Market
Sandpits (The Bedwardine)	Bromyard Road	Vaults	Little Angel Street
Saracen's Head	Tything	Vauxhall	Astwood Road
Sebright Arms	London Road	Vine	Ombersley Road
Seven Stars	Quay Street	Virgin Tavern	Tolladine Road
Shades	Mealcheapen Street	Vulcan	St Pauls Street
Shades	Diglis Street	Washington	Washington Street
Shakespeare	Angel Street	Waterloo	Waterloo Street
Ship	Copenhagen Street	West Midlands Arms	Lowesmoor
Sow and Pigs	Dolday	Wheelwrights Arms	Hylton Road
Star and Garter	Foregate Street	Wheatsheaf	Henwick Road
Star	Bransford Road	Wherry	Quay Street
Star Tap	Farrier Street	White Hart	College Street
Stationer's Arms	High Street	White Horse	Silver Street
Swan	St Johns	White Lion	Lowesmoor Wharf
Swan	Lowesmoor	Wine Vaults	Bridge Street
Swan	Pump Street	Wool Pack	Dolday
		York House	The Moors

1855 Advertisements for LEFT: New Greyhound, and The Bell; RIGHT: Express Tavern and The Eagle Wine Vaults. (All B1855)

LEFT: The Portobello Inn, Bransford Road, St John's c1920, licensee J. Hunt — named from the capture of the Spanish naval base at Porto Bello in Panama in 1739 by Admiral Vernon. (CMH) RIGHT: The Hope & Anchor Hotel at the junction of Newport Street and North Quay, when flooded about 1912; by 1928 the hotel was known as Severn View. (CMH) BELOW: The Old Severn Trow, Quay Street, c1880, licensee R. Roberts. (AG)

LEFT: The Anchor Inn, Lower Bath Road (now called Diglis Road), at the entrance to Diglis Basin; the licensee, seen here about 1900, is Hannah Mason. (KB) RIGHT: The Gun Tavern, Newtown Road c1920, licensee Mrs Ada Potter; Mr Potter is serving drinks through the front bar window, a common practice during the summer months, as the inn had a large front courtyard. Spreckleys, the local brewery, supplied it and beer cost around 6d a pint. The inn takes its name from a rifle range on Ronkswood Hill during the 19th century. (GLC) BELOW:
    At the Old Greyhound c1910: a trick photo, for the same group of four people appear twice. (AP)

ABOVE: Tybridge Street, junction with Hylton Road, 4 March 1926, from with the Bear Inn in the centre. Tybridge Street was once the principal route to the City from the west, as it led directly to the original bridge. (SN/BO'H) BELOW LEFT: Pony and trap at the Old Greyhound Inn, New Street. The girl is Norah Silverthorn, daughter of Harry Silverthorn (on left) who was licensee c1900–1927; Norah married George 'Bert' Fox. (AP) BELOW RIGHT: Wedding at St Martins Church, Cornmarket 1924 of Norah and 'Bert' Fox, who for many years kept the York House, in The Moors. (AP) ABOVE RIGHT: York House in The Moors c1935, showing the 'Green Bar' area. The little girl in the basket is Audrey, daughter of licensee George 'Bert' Fox. (AP)

ABOVE: St Georges' Tavern c1880 with licensee George Cullis, in St Georges Lane, conveniently on the banks of the canal, near the canal bridge, one of the watermen's inns. It is now The Cavalier. BELOW: The Plough Hotel, Silver Street, c1932, proprietor Fred Clarkson, was in the Cornmarket area, and demolished in 1972. (RS) OPPOSITE ABOVE: The Queen's Head inn, c1870, stood at the corner of The Tything and Salt Lane (now Castle Street), and was demolished to widen Salt Lane. The licensee was H. J. Kettle. (HDG) BELOW: The Boat Inn, Lowesmoor, 14 September 1919 and the annual outing to Hereford; the licensee was then Ciss Instan and the site is now the Co-operative Funeral Parlour. (AWW)

LEFT: London Wine and Spirit Vaults, 13 Bridge Street c1890: in the doorway are George Clissold and his daughter Clare, (who married Richard James). (AG) RIGHT: Wine Vaults at 21 Little Angel Street c1900, which became the Vaults Hotel. To the right is Angel Row which led to Lewis Clarke's brewery and Morton Square. The poster in the left doorway announces steamer trips on the 'Castle' line, to Holt and Stourport, and Clare Clissold is in the right hand doorway. (AG) BELOW: Hop picking at Powick c1900. (MS)

ABOVE: Hop picking at Upper House Farm, Suckley, c1900: the two girls kneeling by the bushel basket are the Adams sisters, with Lillian in front and Dolan just behind her and the bushel. (GDP) BELOW: Hop picking at Grove Farm c1929. (SAT)

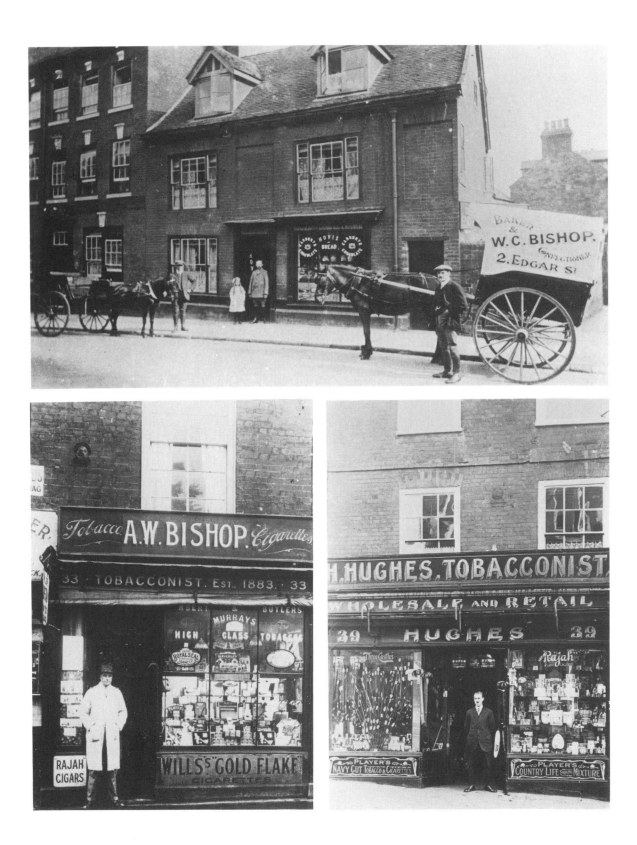

A CITY OF SHOPKEEPERS

For centuries the City had a wealth of small shops and local traders. These were often associated with small manufacturing businesses, producing a wide range of goods, and thereby providing local employment. There was a ready market, and the businesses served not only Worcester's own population, then clustered mostly around the heart of the City, but also people from the surrounding towns and villages. These were the days before the giant chain stores and supermarkets.

The trade directories spanning the years from 1855 to 1937 and old advertisements reflect the enormous range of commodities available and in great popular demand. Visiting many of the shops must have been a highly aromatic experience. Imagine for instance, the bakers, game and fish stalls, feed and grain stores and the spices, fruit, vegetables and tobaccos, all on open display and not 'convenience' wrapped. Sawdust covered the floor at the fishmongers and butchers and there were impressive displays of Severn salmon and great sides of beef and lamb. Besides the dress shops, with yards of cloth, there would have been funeral and mourning warehouses. Cash was placed in small tubular containers and whizzed along wires from one end to the other of large stores, where tills of imposing design rang and jangled. In 1885, one grocery store, that of E. Leonard of 25, Broad Street, offered a huge range of produce, including 32 types of tea, 14 of coffee, 25 of cocoa and chocolate, 12 different sugars, nine kinds of hops and a variety of imported fruits.

During the 1860s the Co-op movement was established in Worcester, but proved unsuccessful at the first attempt. Some twenty years later the movement was re-established. Many traders viewed the Co-op with concern as, under the direction of Mr Manning, the Society established a bakery to provide cheap bread and set out to break the hold of the Millers' and Bakers' Association. Later, the Co-op expanded to grocery and general provisions, occupying a number of sites in the City.

The corner shop was often the focus for a local community. Many are well remembered by older citizens, who readily recall such shops as Fosbury's in Wylds Lane and Jeynes' of Copenhagen Street.

OPPOSITE ABOVE: William Charles Bishop's baker's and confectioner's shop in Edgar Street c1912: with him in the doorway is his daughter, Elsie, and his son Archibald is near the pony and trap. (HDG) LEFT: Archibald William Bishop (known as 'Arch Bishop') in the doorway of his tobacconist and fishing tackle shop at 33 St John's c1930 — Archibald took over the business from George Hambling; next door is the Bell Inn. (HDG) RIGHT: H. Hughes' tobacconist and walking stick shop at 39 St John's c1930 — he was uncle to Archibald Bishop. (HDG)

LEFT: H. R. Cousens' Co-operative Bakery, c1885, with premises at St Swithins Street, 54 St John's and 18 Sidbury, all subsequently occupied by Walter J. Burden's Bakery Company when the Co-op moved elsewhere. (PPs/WCM)

RIGHT: Burden's Bakery at 18 (now 61) Sidbury, c1908: Dorset Dairy butter is advertised for 1s 3d per pound. Later the premises were occupied for many years by Harrison's Antique shop and are now the Antique Map and Print Gallery. (AN/WCM) BELOW: Walter J. Burden and members of his staff at his bakery, along the north side of St Swithins Street (next door, to the right, was Osborne & Sharpes glass and lead merchants) c1903. The business was established here in 1891 and opened branches at St John's, Sidbury and The Tything. By 1912, all premises, except those in St John's, were under the ownership of confectioners Patton and Wells. (WCM)

ABOVE: Burden's 'Model Steam Bakery' and about 100 cottage loaves, c1903, Walter Burden in the dark suit. (AN/WCM) BELOW: Steward's chemist shop at 27 High Street, opposite Copenhagen Street c1905. Established in 1776 by Mr Featherstonehaugh, Mr Walter Woods took over in 1842 and it passed to J. A. Steward in 1874, succeeded by his son C. A. Steward about 1905, and C. C. Steward in 1934. The company sold a wide range of goods, from lamp oil to sheep dips and trusses, and for the poorer folk 'penny' doses of laudanum, while the wealthier had medicines prepared in special red pill boxes and carriage delivered. The business ceased in 1973 and the City Museum acquired the complete shop fittings, putting them on permanent display. The premises are now Russell & Bromleys, shoe shop. (WCM)

LEFT: Steward's 1912 advertisement (L1912) and Lunn's penetrating remedy. (RHGB) RIGHT: ELT's sturdy footwear of 1908 (L1908) and Hooper's delicious sweetmeats. (RHGB)

ABOVE: Dicks Central Boot Stores, 63 High Street, c1925, manufacturers of the 'Perfecta' brand of boot, and now Manfield's Shoe Shop. (MA) BELOW: J.J. Williams & Co, grocers, No 1 The Cross, c1911; eventually became the International Stores, now occupied by the National Westminster Bank. (EFT)

LEFT: Edward Ingles Burgess, newsagent & tobacconist and gents' hairdresser, 3 Angel Street, in December c1906. Christmas cards are advertised in the window at two shillings per dozen and a wash & brush-up for two pence. Until recently the premises were occupied by Lawday's, newsagents. (RS) RIGHT: William Bowcott & Co, cycle agent, at 99½ High Street and Fish Street, c1903, established in 1883 and originally operated from premises in Sidbury. George Frank Parry is standing outside the shop. (PW) BELOW: St John's Post Office at the junction of Bromyard Road c1900 with Sam Horton, sub-postmaster and blacksmith; entrance to the smithy is to the left of A. W. George, boot & shoe shop. The large horseshoe above the doorway can just be seen. Centre of the two shops is a 'V.R.' post box. (SAT)

ABOVE LEFT: Mrs Emma Horton c1890, wife of Sam, mother of Charles and Martha; RIGHT: Sam Horton c1890, St John's sub-postmaster and blacksmith, photographed in the smithy yard; BELOW LEFT: Charles Horton c1890, later a butcher in St John's; CENTRE: Mrs Alice Horton c1885, wife of Charles and mother of Ethel; RIGHT: Alice Horton c1890 in Scottish attire. (All SAT)

OPPOSITE ABOVE: Charles Horton's butcher shop, St John's, (opposite entrance to St John's Church); with Mr Horton and his wife Alice is their daughter Ethel (later to become Ethel Tarran). (SAT) BELOW: Henry Tarran at his butcher's shop at 30 Broad Street (opposite Deansway), with his wife Ethel, c1920. (SAT) ABOVE: Hobday's shops in College Street c1905. No 17 (on the left) is the millinery establishment of Mrs Louisa Hobday, while No 18 is the saddle and harness maker, Edward Hobday, both almost opposite College Precincts. A little further up the street at No 11 was another Hobday business — that of James, who was a wire worker, providing hanging baskets, garden arches, trellisses, etc, originally established in Sansome Street in 1830. (AWW) BELOW: Arthur Johns, General Smithy, 110 London Road, c1880 — at the bottom of the London Road bank, next door to the Cross Keys Inn. Arthur's son, G. V. Johns, took over the smithy between 1908–1915, and the premises were then rebuilt. (CMH)

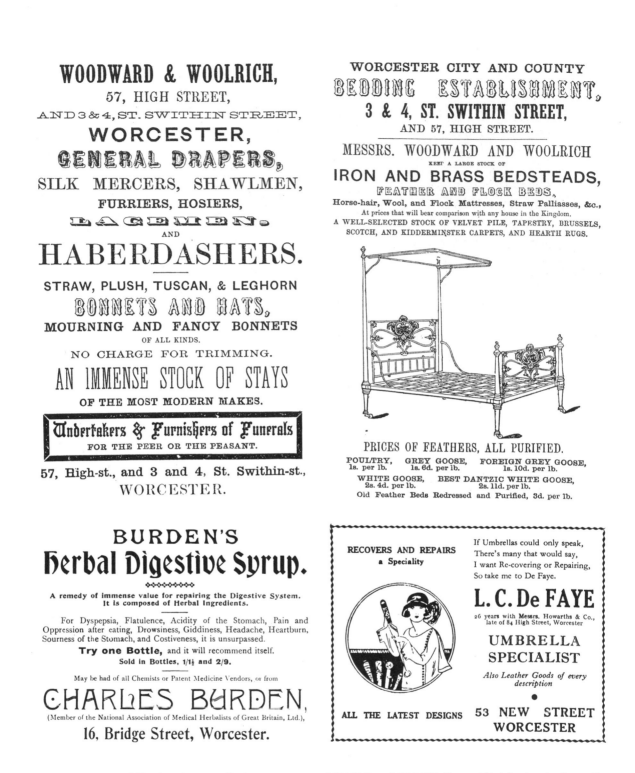

WOODWARD & WOOLRICH,

57, HIGH STREET,

AND 3 & 4, ST. SWITHIN STREET,

WORCESTER,

GENERAL DRAPERS,

SILK MERCERS, SHAWLMEN,

FURRIERS, HOSIERS,

LACEMEN,

AND

HABERDASHERS.

STRAW, PLUSH, TUSCAN, & LEGHORN

BONNETS AND HATS,

MOURNING AND FANCY BONNETS

OF ALL KINDS.

NO CHARGE FOR TRIMMING.

AN IMMENSE STOCK OF STAYS

OF THE MOST MODERN MAKES.

Undertakers & Furnishers of Funerals
FOR THE PEER OR THE PEASANT.

57, High-st., and 3 and 4, St. Swithin-st.,
WORCESTER.

WORCESTER CITY AND COUNTY

BEDDING ESTABLISHMENT,

3 & 4, ST. SWITHIN STREET,

AND 57, HIGH STREET.

MESSRS. WOODWARD AND WOOLRICH

KEEP A LARGE STOCK OF

IRON AND BRASS BEDSTEADS,

FEATHER AND FLOCK BEDS,

Horse-hair, Wool, and Flock Mattresses, Straw Palliasses, &c.,
At prices that will bear comparison with any house in the Kingdom.
A WELL-SELECTED STOCK OF VELVET PILE, TAPESTRY, BRUSSELS,
SCOTCH, AND KIDDERMINSTER CARPETS, AND HEARTH RUGS.

PRICES OF FEATHERS, ALL PURIFIED.

POULTRY,   GREY GOOSE,   FOREIGN GREY GOOSE,
1s. per lb.   1s. 6d. per lb.   1s. 10d. per lb.
WHITE GOOSE,   BEST DANTZIC WHITE GOOSE,
2s. 4d. per lb.   2s. 11d. per lb.
Old Feather Beds Redressed and Purified, 3d. per lb.

BURDEN'S

Herbal Digestive Syrup.

A remedy of immense value for repairing the Digestive System.
It is composed of Herbal Ingredients.

For Dyspepsia, Flatulence, Acidity of the Stomach, Pain and
Oppression after eating, Drowsiness, Giddiness, Headache, Heartburn,
Sourness of the Stomach, and Costiveness, it is unsurpassed.

Try one Bottle, and it will recommend itself.
Sold in Bottles, 1/1½ and 2/9.

May be had of all Chemists or Patent Medicine Vendors, or from

CHARLES BURDEN,

(Member of the National Association of Medical Herbalists of Great Britain, Ltd.),

16, Bridge Street, Worcester.

RECOVERS AND REPAIRS
a Speciality

If Umbrellas could only speak,
There's many that would say,
I want Re-covering or Repairing,
So take me to De Faye.

L. C. De FAYE

26 years with Messrs. Howarths & Co.,
late of 84 High Street, Worcester

UMBRELLA
SPECIALIST

*Also Leather Goods of every
description*

●

ALL THE LATEST DESIGNS

53 NEW STREET
WORCESTER

ABOVE LEFT: 1855 advertisement for 'peer or peasant' (B1855) and RIGHT: for purified feather beds — all
from Woodward and Woolrich. (B1855)   BELOW LEFT: Alternative medicine is not a modern
phenomenon (RHGB) and RIGHT: in 1935 you could stay out of the wet with Mr de Faye. (K1935)

ABOVE: John Albert Fosbury's grocery shop at 59 Wylds Lane at the corner of Great Park Street c1890; left, Mr Fosbury snr, John Fosbury wearing the apron. In the doorway is Miss Kate Fosbury who eventually owned the business and married Bertie Ayliffe. (JAG) BELOW: Ayliffe family group at Fort Royal Hill c1905. (JAG)

The Ayliffe family owned a shop at the corner of Fort Royal Hill and Wylds Lane, opposite Fosbury's. ABOVE LEFT: Mrs Amelia Ayliffe in 1912; RIGHT: Harry Ayliffe c1912; BELOW LEFT: Emily Ayliffe c1912 and RIGHT: Carrie Ayliffe, (became Carrie Ottey). JAG)

SPORTS AND SOCIAL

Sports of all descriptions have abounded in the City. In the 18th century 'gaming' practices such as cock fighting took place at many City inns, where commoners and gentry met for great tournaments: a 'main of cocks'. These contests lasted for hours, with vast amounts of money changing hands. A more elegant pastime would have been a game of bowls on one of the many greens.

Public houses were often the venue for these sports, the Pheasant in New Street hosting both with a cock fighting 'pit' and bowling green. The most select bowling green in the City, where the fashionable were to be seen during the 18th century, was at the Saracen's Head.

Team sports were always popular and it seems that almost every parish boasted a football and a cricket team. The Worcester City Football Club was formed by the amalgamation of two strong teams, Worcester Rovers and Berwick Rangers, largely through the efforts of local sportsman Harry Smith. Early this century the Clubs' HQ was in the Old Peacock Inn, Queen Street. The Club Secretary, Harry Yoxall, was also the publican.

Pitchcroft has been the scene of many sporting and public events. There were the bare knuckle prize fights of the 19th century, and in particular the famous Spring and Langan fight of 1824. This was fought over 84 rounds for the Championship of England and was watched by a crowd estimated at some 40,000. After two hours 23 minutes, Spring was declared the victor. Pitchcroft was also the setting for the fairs and circuses which were usually preceded by spectacular and colourful parades. An alternative site was on meadows along New Road, adjacent to Bromwich Road. Many other parades took place in the City, particularly those of carnivals, election 'bandwagons' and 'Lifeboat Saturdays'. These were great popular occasions, attended by much good humour and by some of the many local characters.

The river was a natural magnet for sport. The Ariel Boat Club, established in 1841, saw the beginnings of competitive rowing in Worcester, and the Worcester Rowing Club was formed in 1876. Swimming barges were moored to the banks of the Severn near Pitchcroft and many learnt to swim in their murky waters. During the 1930s a 'mile' race was held for swimmers, down the river from Kepax to the Grandstand. A more comfortable alternative was the open air Baths in Sansome Walk. Originally built and opened by Mr Barber of Cheltenham in 1854, the Lett family acquired the property during the 1860s. This building, with its elegant portico complete with two caryatids, passed to Charles Bartholemew in 1878. Turkish baths proved most popular, as did more exotic forms of bath such as sulphur, iodine, salt, calomel, 'electric' and Bartholemew's own 'nature cure'. William Park took over the baths in 1889, and they continued under the management of his son, Leonard. Eventually they were demolished, to be replaced in 1972 with an indoor complex on the site.

Family excursions were often to the river, either to cross *via* one of the four ferries located at the Cathedral, Grandstand, Dog and Duck or Kepax, or to enjoy a trip on one of the many steamers, upstream or down.

ABOVE: St Stephen's Football Club. (JAG) BELOW: Comer Villa Football Club. (RFJ)

ABOVE: Worcester City FC 1924–5, Champions 1st Division, Birmingham League. (JAG) BELOW; Royal Oak Football Club c1910. (JC)

ABOVE: St Clement's Football Club, 1911–12. (GC) BELOW: St John's Football Club, 1911–12. (GC)

ABOVE: Briggs Brothers Football team, 1920s: back row, L to R: George, Charlie, Ken; middle row: Sid, Fred, Arthur; front row: Harry, Eddie, Martin (with ball), Ernie, Harvey. (WPB) BELOW: A cricket team outside Chapel in Castle Street c1885; the boy on the right is Henry Swan Brown, born 8 September 1877. (LG)

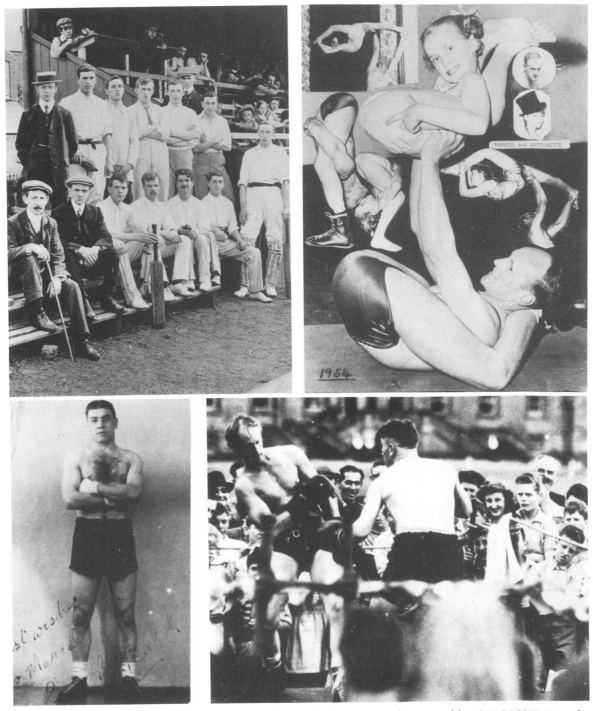

ABOVE LEFT: St Martin's Cricket Club, 1908; in the stand a boy writes at the score table. (CH) RIGHT: Marcel Callow and his daughter Antoinette were celebrated acro-contortionists who appeared locally and toured nationally and internationally. Their double act began in 1950 and continued for some 15 years. (MKCA) BELOW LEFT: Geoff Heath c1950 — a successful local middleweight boxer. (MKCA) RIGHT: Marcel Callow vs Geoff Heath; an open-air exhibition fight at Croome Court c1946. Among the audience were children from the Royal Albert Orphanage. (MKCA)

ABOVE: Worcester Weight Lifting and Physical Culture Club, c1935, with Bert Floyd of Tybridge Street second from left, middle row. (HDG) BELOW: Worcester City & County Harriers, 1899, outside Showell's Lansdown Hotel, Lowesmoor Place. (LT)

OPPOSITE ABOVE: Circus parade in the Cornmarket, c1900; two elephants pull a cart with a skeleton of one of their forebears. (EFT) CENTRE: John Sanger's Circus, c1890. (JJC/AJB) BELOW: The lions' cage on Pitchcroft during the visit of a circus, c1890. (EFT) ABOVE: All the fun of the fair: Booth's Rocket Ride, c1870. (FCE/HC) BELOW: Boxing booth and 'Don't forget to see the pretty girls of Paris now on view. A thing of beauty is a joy forever', at the fair.

ABOVE: An early bi-plane on Pitchcroft c1912 — the scene of many early pioneering flights and not without danger. In 1910 Mrs Ellen Pitt was killed when a Bleriot machine swerved into crowds lining the take-off route, after rising a few feet off the ground. The German aviator, Gustav Hamil (or Hummel) flew here in 1913–14. (RS) CENTRE: Baby Week, 5 July 1917 on Pitchcroft; the lady with the small pram, left of centre, is Mrs Agnes Taylor, from Astwood Road, with her daughter, Mary. (AB) BELOW: Cottage Homes New Scouts, with members of Cottage Homes Committee, Midland Road, 9 July 1929. (EJH/RH)

ABOVE: Worcester 'F' Troop Boy Scouts, in action with a fire tender near canal side, c1903. (MP) BELOW: Boys' Brigade, c1930. (EJH/RH)

ABOVE: The Globe Hotel Angling Society, winners of the Worcester Knockout, and the Rigden Cup, 1934–1935. (KB) BELOW: Skating on the Severn during a severe frost in the 1880s; the ice was thick enough to support traders' stalls and an ox roast. (JC/AJB)

ABOVE: Worcester Rowing Club and boat house, c1915. (RS) INSET: Charles Webb, attendant at the Bathing Barge on the Severn, during the early 1900s. (AG) BELOW: Bartholomew's (later Park's) Baths, Sansome Walk, c1885. (LWP)

ABOVE: The Dog and Duck ferry, c1935, at the north end of Pitchcroft; its name originates in the watermans' inn on the west bank, and the Sunday morning 'sport' of betting on dogs which were loosed on the river to catch a duck, after its wing tendons were cut. (WCM) BELOW: Kepax ferry with Kepax House, c1900; it was sometimes known as 'Bailey's Boat'. (CMH)

ABOVE: Three Castle Line steamers at the South Quay, c1912: the *Holt Castle* is on the left, then the largest steamer on the Severn, with a capacity for 326; the middle vessel is the *Avonmore Castle* carrying 230 and on the right, the smaller *Hanley Castle* for 50 passengers. Other notable steamers at Worcester included *The Severn* and the *Lady Alwyn* in the 1880s and, in the 1920s, *The Beatrice, Star* and *Dove*, and the *Duchess of York* owned by George Williams, built in teak and licensed to carry 167 passengers. This vessel was renamed *The Duchess Doreen* in the 1920s. (RS) BELOW: *The Perseverance* at Holt Fleet, c1890, was launched in 1868 near the railway bridge from Stevens' Yard. Originally built as a paddle steamer and later converted to screw drive, powered by two 10 hp engines, she was 91 feet long and 14 feet wide, and her last trip was in 1904. She was converted into a boathouse near Warmstry Slip for Frank Roberts, who owned the Castle Line, before being broken up during the 1950s. (WCM)

ABOVE: One of Worcester's favourite steamers *The Belle*, about 1911, with a party from Willis' shoe factory, on a trip to Holt Fleet. The little girl to the left of the upper deck is Violet Griffiths, with her parents; *The Belle* was brought to Worcester by Harry Everton in 1896, after a voyage round the coast from London and up the Severn. (VS) BELOW: Harry Everton and Annie Finlinson: wedding day in January 1896, photographed in Comer Road, St John's, Worcester. (EG)

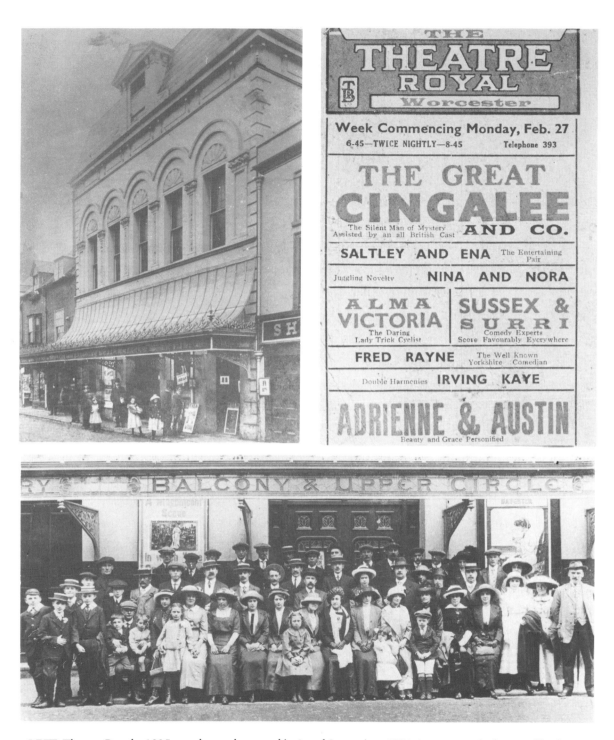

LEFT: Theatre Royal, c1905 — a theatre has stood in Angel Street since 1779; it was severely damaged by fire in 1912, and extensively reconstructed, then demolished in 1962. Kwik Save supermarket is now upon the site. (RS) RIGHT: Theatre Royal playbill. (KB) BELOW: Theatre Royal and Empire Cinema (Foregate Street) staff outing, 1913. (RS)

ABOVE: The Worcester Orchestra at the Public Hall, c1925; among the musicians are: Mr J. Phipps, cello; Mrs Phipps, violin; Mr R. Phipps, clarinet. (WWH/DEP) BELOW: Black and White Minstrel Group, c1900. (AG)

ABOVE: Cinderella Works (J. F. Willis & Co, Watery Lane) Kazoo Band, c1931; formed by Mrs Atkinson (7th from right, front row) and Mr Allen, a foreman (on left hand side). The Managing Director, Mr Henry James Marrian, is centre rear of picture. Others in the picture include Henry Mattocks, Works Manager (R H side), Doris Dowding next to him (middle row), Dorothy Tyrer (extreme left), Ada Mann (directly below Mr Marrian) and Hilda Jarvis (4th from right, back row). Uniforms: red tops with white trousers. (DRH) BELOW: Election Meeting, c1908: the banner proclaims 'Vote for Goulding and have more work and food' and 'Goulding's our man'. Two men are holding two cottage loaves aloft on poles. (DB)

ABOVE: Worcester Baptist Chapel Indian Club Club. (EJH/RH) BELOW: Carnival float in the 1920s on Heenan & Froude lorry; the railway lines in the foreground suggest the picture was taken at the factory in Shrub Hill Road. (FHu)

LEFT: Nobby Guy was a well known Worcester character of the 1930s, who often unofficially led civic processions, and would also jump off Worcester Bridge – if offered enough money. (AG) RIGHT: Harry Adams, City Bellman, c1885; acting as Town Crier, he gave announcements in the City central area. (HAEH) BELOW: Lifeboat Saturday, 25 September, 1909, at the junction of Sansome Street and Lowesmoor, with the Old Falcon Inn on the right; Pickford's warehouse is in the centre, with Caswell's noted tea and coffee rooms, just left of the boat, adjacent to Chas E. Brown's monumental sculpture business. Lifeboat Saturday was a regular annual event in the City during the second half of the 19th and early 20th centuries. In 1867 *The City of Worcester* was launched at Bembridge, Isle of Wight, provided by the citizens of Worcester; it rowed 10 sets of oars and saved some 24 lives. (FHB)

FROM PEDALS TO PETROL

One of the great social revolutions of the 19th century was brought about by the introduction of the 'cycle. In both Victorian and Edwardian eras, 'cycling proved a great attraction. It allowed ordinary folk to travel long distances at relatively little cost. Many clubs were formed, and their members were often seen trundling *en-masse* along leafy lanes and narrow by-ways to a favourite resort, usually associated with a tavern.

In the late 1800s the City boasted about a dozen manufacturers of machines and as many bicycle and tricycle clubs. Groups of enthusiasts often wore military-looking uniforms and communicated along the length of the mobile column by blowing a bugle or whistle to give coded messages. There was a strict code of conduct and recommendations were given with regard to the manner of overtaking horses. Protocol was observed, too, with the captain heading the procession and the sub captain bringing up the rear. To overtake the captain was considered a major offence.

Some clubs were purely social and many were associated with factories. Others developed into sporting clubs, St John's being a notable example. Early clubs in the City included the Bicycle and Tricycle Club, YMCA, Royal Porcelain, St John's, Worcester Road, City and County Wheel Club (which was open to ladies), Clarion, Co-operative, the City Wheelers, and St George's.

Another invention which had far-reaching consequences for the life of the City was that of the motor car. First only a few were to be seen in the streets of Worcester, but before long local manufacturers began to provide for the needs of motorists and several 'dealers' were established. In 1908, there were about ten dealers and garages. One company still survives today, Bladder's in Sidbury, whereas a manufacturer, McNaught & Co, is only commemorated by McNaught Place.

Besides the principal manufacturers, many small companies produced 'cycle cars' for cheap motoring without frills. These little cars were usually powered by a two cylinder motorcycle engine. Most of the manufacturers of 'cycle cars eventually went out of business, but one notable firm which remains from those early days is the Morgan Company of Malvern.

OPPOSITE ABOVE: Worcester Tricycle Club in action during the great cycle craze of the 1880s, and BELOW: resting. (JJC/AJB)

ABOVE: Having parked their machines, the Tricycle Club are ready to take photographs with the plate camera mounted on a wooden tripod. (JJC/AJB) BELOW: Fownes Gloves Cycling Club during the 'Society' cycling boom late last century. (WCM)

ABOVE LEFT: Ernie Payne, The Worcester Wonder, rode for Britain in the 1908 Olympics; he was a member of St John's Cycle Club. (WCM) RIGHT: An early car on Old Hills; the large radiator is an addition to the original design. (JJC/AJB) CENTRE LEFT: A typical town car c1910–12, and a painful looking 'accident'. (JAB) RIGHT: Frank Brettell, driving a Lanchester in Battenhall Road c1907; he was a cornbroker. (JOB) BELOW LEFT: Mr H. N. Gray, fruit merchant, with one of the first motor cars seen in the City, a Studebaker. (AG) RIGHT: A Standard car at Old Greyhound Yard, probably in the 1920s. (AP)

ABOVE: A motor car outing at the Old Greyhound, c1905, with two Wolseleys centre. (AP) BELOW: A. F. Tansell's garage at 30/32 Bath Road, c1928; Albert Frank Tansell established his first garage under one of the railway arches near the Butts, then the business moved to 52 London Road (opposite the Fort Royal Inn) in 1921. In 1926 he exchanged premises with Cecil Marks, proprietor of Marks' Blue Coach Services, who had his garage at 30/32 Bath Road. Tansells moved to their present site in Diglis Road in 1932. The Bath Road premises were then taken over by T. J. Daniels, who subsequently sold out to George Humphries, who named the garage 'The Motor House'. Bristol Street Motors occupy the site today. (DT) OPPOSITE LEFT: F. Sanders' Cycle & Motor business at 6 Barbourne Road, next door to the Talbot Inn, in 1908 was one of twelve such in the City; established in 1893, they also had a bicycle riding school. (RH) RIGHT: An early AA Patrol. (RS) BELOW: William Shuard on a JAP Motor Cycle outside St Stephen's Vicarage, c1930. (RS)

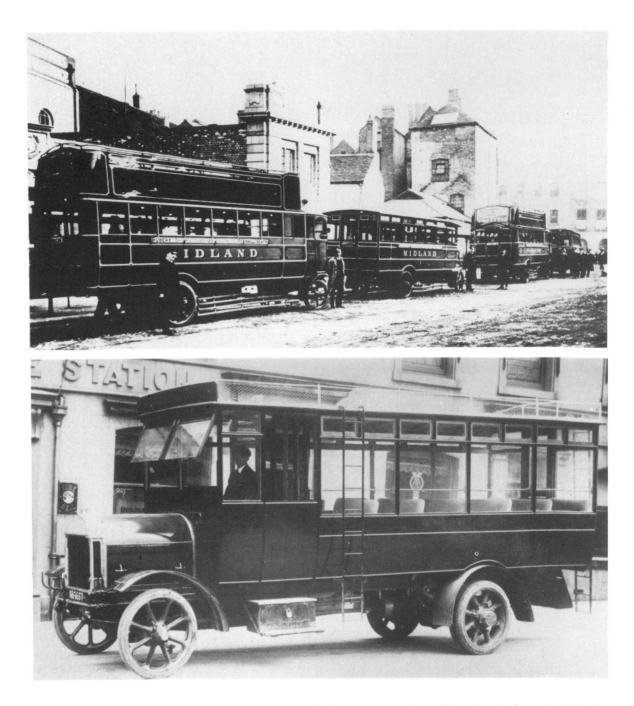

ABOVE: Two double-deck open top, and two single-deck motor coaches of the Birmingham & Midland Omnibus Company Ltd at Angel Place c1922; the destination of the left hand 'bus was Rubery, via Bromsgrove, Droitwich and Fernhill Heath. (AGJ/HWCA) BELOW: Motor omnibus AB3657 at Five Ways, outside the Norwich Union offices of Watkins & Sayce; it was operated by Owen's Motor Service to Pensax, Abberley and Witley. (CMH)

CRIME AND PUNISHMENT

There have been several prisons at Worcester throughout the centuries. The Bridewell, in Copenhagen Street, which accommodated mainly women (often with children), served as an early form of workhouse, closing when the House of Industry (Hillborough) opened on Tallow Hill in the 18th century. The gatehouse to the Foregate in the City walls, which stood until slighted by Cromwell's orders, also provided prison cells. There were cells too, beneath the Guildhall, a lock-up in the yard, and cells in the ancient fortification on Castle Hill. Most of these were fairly temporary or created through expediency. It was not until 1824 that the City had its first purpose-built Gaol. It was erected in Friar Street at the junction with Union Street and cost £12,578. It held between 30 and 40 prisoners and was equipped with a treadmill. Until its closure in 1867 it had only one Governor, William Griffiths.

The County Gaol stood in Castle Street. Built in 1813, its fortified appearance resulted in the name of the street being changed from Salt Lane to Castle Street. Established with 90 cells, it was enlarged by a further 80 in 1839, at the time of the Chartist agitation.

Public hangings and whippings occurred in Castle Street until 1863. The list of executions at the Gaol makes interesting, if somewhat gruesome, reading. The range of offences that carried capital punishment was wide, and the ages of offenders sometimes very tender, as the following examples illustrate.

1800. At the Summer Assizes, thirteen persons were sentenced to death, and three of them executed – one for burglary, and two for sheep stealing.

1801. At the Lent Assizes five persons were sentenced to death for burglary; one was hanged.

March, 1803. Richard Colledge was executed for horse stealing.

June, 1803. Thomas Beach was executed for uttering a forged £5 note.

March 23, 1821. Thomas Dyer, capitally convicted of horse stealing, was executed at the County Gaol, but died protesting his entire innocence of the crime laid to his charge.

August 24, 1821. William Mantle and William Bird were executed at the County Gaol, the former convicted of stealing sheep, the property of Mr Henry Hyde, of Little Kyre, and the latter of breaking into the house of Mr John Bird, of Bromsgrove, and stealing wearing apparel, etc. The ropes were nearly extended to their full length when tied round the unhappy culprits' necks, so that scarcely any fall took place, and they died in great agony, especially Bird. Their remains were interred in St. Andrew's churchyard.

March 31, 1830. Michael Toll, convicted of the wilful murder of Ann Cook, a woman with whom he lived, by knocking her into a pit at Oldswinford, was executed this day in front of the County Gaol. His body was given to the surgeons to anatomise, and afterwards exposed to public gaze at the Infirmary.

July 30, 1830. Charles Wall, convicted at the Summer Assizes of the murder of Sally Chance, at Oldswinford, was executed in front of the County Prison at six o'clock pm, the execution having been deferred to that unusual hour in consequence of the election taking place that day. His body was delivered to a surgeon at Stourbridge, and afterwards exposed to view to great crowds who came from all the surrounding parts to see it.

March 25, 1831. Thomas Slaughter, a lad not eighteen years of age, was executed for setting fire to a large wheat rick, the propery of Mrs Rebecca Tomlinson, of Elmley Lovett. The poor fellow was wholly uneducated, and evidently of weak intellect.

March 22, 1832. James and Joseph Carter, two brothers, aged twenty and twenty-two respectively, who were condemned at the Lent Assizes for two cases of highway robbery at night, with violence, in the neighbourhood of Bewdley, this morning underwent the extreme penalty of the law in front of the County Gaol. Both men met death with firmness, but without bravado; and Joseph Carter addressed the populace from the scaffolding.

January 2, 1863. William Ockold was executed for the murder of his wife at Oldbury. This was the last public execution.

(WDT)
1905

Worcester City Gaol, when in use as almshouses, c1880, at the junction of Friar Street and Union Street. The City Gaol, which housed some 30 to 40 prisoners and a treadmill, was in use from 1824 until 1867, when the City and County Gaols were merged. William Laslett then bought the site for his almshouses. For some forty years, the old couples lived in the converted cells until 1912 when the 'Tudor' style Lasletts Almshouses were opened. (WC)

ABOVE: The County Gaol, Castle Street, from the south-east, c1920; the castle-like frontage is clearly shown, together with the cell blocks, high walls and chapel. Love's Grove is to the right, with the Royal Infirmary to the left. (CMH) LEFT: The scene of 'The Worcester Tragedy', 31 The Moors. (CG) RIGHT: Annie 'Tipity Toe Nance' Yarnold, aged 43 years, was stabbed to death by her husband William, outside her cottage in The Moors on 4 October 1905. Before she died, Annie stated that, during her marriage, she was brutally treated by William and he knew she supported him by prostitution. He had threatened her life previously and, upon his return from serving with the Army in South Africa, under the name of Collins, he had become jealous of her living with another man, George Miles. They met briefly at the Hope and Anchor. The following day, on her doorstep, he stabbed her in the back. Yarnold was found guilty and hanged at Worcester County Gaol, Castle Street, at 7.30 am on 5 December 1905. (WDE)

ABOVE: Members of 3rd Battallion Worcestershire Regiment 1901, winners of the Goldsmiths & Silversmiths Cup for Marksmanship. (WCM) BELOW: Volunteers marching along Barbourne Road, passing the junction with Hebb Street in 1914; it is believed that these men, who had not as yet received proper uniforms or weapons, due to war scarcities, were to form the back-up for the 2nd 8th Battalion of Worcestershire Regiment. (RS)

CITY AT WAR

The City's involvement with the two World Wars was not one of great physical contact, and few scars were suffered from either conflict. At the personal level, the situation was very different, as many volunteered to serve in the armed forces and hundreds lost their lives, or were injured. A glance at the Roll of Honour of the Worcestershire Regiment reveals the extent of their sacrifice.

The valiant exploits of the Regiment have confirmed its place in military history. 'The Gallant Worcesters' gained this name after their exploit at Gheluvelt near Ypres. They were further distinguished by their part in the action at Gallipoli and Katia, and in 1917 the Victoria Cross was awarded to Private Frederick Dancox of the Worcestershire Regiment, who came from Dolday.

Rev Geoffrey Studdert Kennedy, better known as 'Woodbine Willie', was often in the thick of the action in the front line and was awarded the Military Cross. He gained his nickname from offering Woodbine cigarettes and Bibles to men departing for the Front. A powerful orator, he was Vicar of the Parish of St Paul's, one of the most deprived areas in the City, from 1914 to 1922. In the City there were always shortages and people were regularly to be seen queuing for hours to obtain general provisions.

During the Second World War, Worcester was nominated as a 'target' by the Germans. Luftwaffe photographs show designated target areas at Diglis, where there were petrol storage tanks, and at Norton Barracks. The citizens took air-raid precautions and shelters were constructed in the streets, gas masks carried as standard items and parts of the Cathedral bricked up. Home Guard units were established, with their HQ in Silver Street, while Civil Defence was based at Hounds Lane School, and 'black-out' became familiar, as did the patrols of ARP Wardens.

In 1940, two incidents occurred to bring home the harsh realities of war to the City. On the night of 7 September, five bombs fell on the Tallow Hill area, close to Shrub Hill Station and Hillborough, where the HQ of 81 Group Fighter Command was located. On 3 October, a lone German raider swept low, to drop two bombs on the Meco factory in Bromyard Road, killing seven and injuring sixty.

During the war the City had its own RAF airfield at Perdiswell, from which 81 Group Fighter Command operated. Later Perdiswell served as a training airfield and De Havilland Tiger Moths became a common sight, flying over the rooftops.

In 1942 a Douglas DC3 Dakota, bearing the inscription 'Idiot's Delight', and carrying General Spaatz of the US Army Air Corps, attempted a landing at Perdiswell. The aircraft aquaplaned on the wet runway, overshot, and came to rest across Bilford Road with its nose almost in the rubbish tip. Spaatz broke his foot in the incident and remarked 'I came all this way just to end up in a trash heap!'.

Worcester welcomed scores of children evacuated from Birmingham, and also served as host to many American GIs, visiting the City from their wartime base at Blackmore Camp near Malvern. In this way 131 local girls came to know the GIs very well and became 'GI brides'.

123

LEFT: Reverend Geoffery Anketell Studdert Kennedy, 'Woodbine Willie', the legendary World War I padre and poet. Here is just one graphic stanza: 'Waste of blood, and waste of tears, Waste of youth's most precious years, Waste of ways the saints have trod, Waste of glory, waste of God – War!' He was Vicar of the poor parish of St Paul in the Blockhouse district, 1914–1922. He died on 8 March 1929, after 'flu' and asthma had developed rapidly into pneumonia, and his loss was mourned nationwide; he is buried in St John's cemetery. (RE)
RIGHT: Queueing for provisions during World War I at the corner of Charles Street and Pump Street; the building in the background is the Charles Street Assembly Rooms. (VS) BELOW: Collecting potatoes from James' Meat, Potato & Fruit shop in Pump Street, during World War I; the public house to the left of the shop is the Horse & Jockey and James' shop is now Tyler's radio and TV business, opposite the Shambles. (AG)

Great Britain and Ireland.

Army Form B. 55.

Applicable only during the emergency commencing on 4th August, 1914.

To the OCCUPIER (name) *Mrs Goodman*

(See Note A)

at *47 Chestnut* Street, in the Parish of *Worcester*

In accordance with the provisions of the Army Act you are hereby required to find Quarters for—

OFFICERS AND MEN—

Class I.	.... Lodging and Attendance for _____ officers ___1___ men
Class II.	.... Lodging and Attendance for __X__ men
Class III.	.... Unfurnished Accommodation for _____ officers _____ men

The Military Authorities are empowered to call upon you to provide meals as well as quarters for soldiers.

HORSES—

Class I. .... Proper Stabling with forage for _____ horses

Class II. .... Proper Stabling without forage for _____ horses

Class III. ..... Covered Accommodation only for _____ horses

of the _____ Regiment, from _____ to _____ (if period known).

Dated the *1st* day of *April* 19*19*

HB Noughrient. Billet Master.

Overleaf are shown :—

The accommodation to be provided under each class.

The quantities of food and drink to be supplied to soldiers (if you are required to supply meals) as fixed by His Majesty's Regulations.

The rates of payment for accommodation, meals, etc.

NOTE A.—In time of national emergency the occupiers of all public buildings, dwelling-houses, warehouses, barns, and stables are, as well as the keepers of victualling houses, liable to provide billets, with or without meals.

(6203) W 12223/R1020 1,500,000 12/16 McA. & W., Ltd. (E. 741) [P.T.O.

ABOVE: Army form B55 for billetting of officers and men at the home of Mrs Goodman at 47 Chestnut Street in 1919. Elsewhere the form makes financial allowances for meals and accommodation and has the interesting footnote 'G' – 'The manure remains the property of the War Department, which is entitled to any benefit arising from its disposal'. (RFJ) LEFT: Worcester's 'Tank Bank' *Julian*, 18 March 1918, outside the Cathedral, assisted as an attraction for raising War Funds. (WWH/WC) RIGHT: A 'captured' German bi-plane on display outside the Cathedral, opposite College Street/Lich Street, on 18 March 1918. (WWH)

ABOVE: Excerpt from 'Roll of Honour' in *Berrows Illustrated Supplement*, 11 November 1916. (BW J/BC)
BELOW: Battenhall Mount (now St Mary's Convent School) was used as a VAD hospital and sanatorium during World War I; c1917. (WWH/RS)

126

Sex. MALE   Height 5·9½

Eyes HAZEL   Hair DARK BROWN

Date of Birth 2nd APRIL 1922

Visible Distinguishing Marks.

SCAR TOP OF TONGUE.

DECLARATION—I DECLARE that I have personal knowledge, extending over.............years (months) of the person to whom this Identity Card relates, that the signature within is his (her) true signature, that he (she) possesses the above physical characteristics and has stated to me the above date of his (her) birth:

(★) and that the photograph above, signed by me is a true likeness of that person.

Signed Henry German   Date 12/11/43

Service or Employment of Declarant. S/Lt N.F.S

IDENTIFICATION PARTICULARS

ABOVE: Worcestershire Regiment parading through Lowesmoor 1937–38; Mr George Bethel in left file, with white arm band, played the side drum: they are passing by the Alma Inn, Poole's Fried Fish Shop, right and at the extreme right, Reginald E. Pritchett's fruit shop. (AGB) BELOW: A Second World War National Identity Card No DJ912425 . (WHK)

ABOVE: AFS personnel, Friday night Team. Standing L to R: Len Knight, Harry Robinson, Lawrence Ayling; seated L to R: Bill King, B. Pratt, Bill Callow and Jack Morris. At first they met at Bull Entry and the Central Fire Station and then London Road/Victoria Avenue. (WHK) BELOW: Deansway from the north (Birdport area); 1943 Wings for Victory Parade. Civil Defence Units march past a Halifax Bomber on the future site of the Technical College, the Duke of Wellington public house on the left, demolished in the 1970s, and St Andrew's Church on the right. (WEN/HWCA)

ABOVE: Members of the Worcestershire Regiment dressed as German soldiers took part in two Second World War propaganda films: *The Foreman Went to France* and *Next of Kin*. (AGB) CENTRE: A Douglas DC3 Dakota 17736 *Idiots Delight* which, when carrying the US General Spaats, overshot Perdiswell and crashed on Bilford Road in 1942. (GL) BELOW: VE Day party in Crown Street 1945; the girl on the extreme right is Valerie Edwards. (PB)

THE RAILWAY REVOLUTION

Despite encouragement from Brunel himself, Worcester was slow to become involved with railway schemes. Passengers for London purchased tickets at the booking office at the Crown Hotel in Broad Street, whence they were conveyed by carriage to the City's nearest railway station at Spetchley. It was only in 1850 that the Oxford, Worcester and Wolverhampton line (O W & W) was connected to Worcester. The O W & W was in considerable financial difficulties and was poorly organised, often referred to as the 'Old Worse and Worse' line. The situation improved dramatically with the appointment of Alexander Clunes Sherriff (who gave his name to Sherriff Street) to manage the line from Shrub Hill. The O W & W became the West Midland Railway, which in turn was absorbed by the Great Western Railway (G W R). Worcester soon became a railway centre with Shrub Hill (1865), and the huge shunting yards, sheds and the great engine works in Shrub Hill Road (in later years occupied by Heenan and Froudes). Until the viaduct was opened across the Severn, passengers for Malvern and Hereford were obliged to embark from Henwick Station.

In the mid-19th century a major local project was to connect the Docks at Diglis to the main railway line, by a 'spur line' running alongside the river. The intention was to make the City a great inland port once again, by attracting large merchant ships. Much of the line was actually constructed, with a series of descending arches carrying the line from Foregate Street Station, to a point near the Grandstand at Pitchcroft, and continuing along the side of North Quay through an archway at the side of Gwynn's 1781 river bridge, to the South Quay. Here the project stopped, as the Cathedral authorities refused permission for the line to proceed past the Cathedral. The 'Butts spur line' or 'Butts siding' as it was known, served industrial premises along the riverside, moved cattle to market and took goods from small ships on the South Quay. A solitary crane was about as much 'dockland' as the City was to see. In connection with the widening of the bridge in 1932, the line south of the bridge was taken up. The northern section remained until 1957.

OPPOSITE ABOVE: At Worcester Engine Works: engine No 237 was designed by R. Peacock for the Manchester, Sheffield and Lincolnshire Railway and built in September 1852 by R. Stephenson & Co (No 835) at a cost of £2,500. As No 110 *Himalaya*, it was sold to the Oxford, Worcester and Wolverhampton Railway on 29 September 1854 to become their No 37. Although built originally as a tender engine, it was rebuilt by the GWR as 0-6-0 saddle tank No 237 in October 1865, when this photograph was probably taken. (WCM) CENTRE: The original railway bridge, north side c1860; the wooden structure was to strengthen the bridge after Colonel Yolland, the Government Inspector, found fault with the cast iron spans. (TBC) BELOW: The railway bridge, north side, after the arches had been replaced by a straight girder span in 1904. (DP)

ABOVE: This engine, entering Shrub Hill Station from Hereford, is probably No 427, an 0-6-0 outside frame tender engine, standard goods class, built in October 1868 at Swindon and withdrawn in September 1917. To the left is an 0-4-2 tank engine 517 class, bound for Bromyard, with the Loco Sheds in the background, to the right, c1910. (RS) BELOW: Railwaymen at Shrub Hill c1912; Mr Jack Hinett, a plate layer, is standing second from right. (JL)

LEFT: John Vale, who was an inspector with the GWR, and based at Shrub Hill, came from a 'railway family', and grew his beard to cover a sabre cut received during the First World War. (AV) RIGHT: No 1661 on the 'Vinegar Line' across Pheasant Street; the unique signal post carried two signals at right angles to each other, one for the rail and one for the road traffic. Here, once, a steam roller collided with an engine, and the steam roller lost! In operation until the 1960s, the trains ran daily from Hill Evans Vinegar Works to Shrub Hill Station with laden vans from the 'works'. The engine is an 0-6-0 Pannier tank fitted with Spark Arrestor in the chimney. (REJ-R) BELOW: Shrub Hill railway station, complete with glazed roof; this large span was removed during the 1930s. (DP)

ABOVE: Horse tram in Bransford Road, at the junction with Little Boughton Street, c1900. (CMH) BELOW: Horse trams in St John's, near the entrance (right) to the tram depôt, c1900; the shop immediately next door is that of Walter W. Grundy, a butcher with another branch at 30 Broad Street, and next door at No 8 is Mrs R. Daniels, milliner and fancy draper. (CMH)

TRACK AND SIEGE

Established in 1884, the horse trams in Worcester revolutionised the City's transport system. These horse trams, each of which could carry about forty passengers, ran on three-foot gauge tracks, single-line, with a few passing 'loops'. The service operated along two routes: Portobello Inn, Bransford Road *via* the Cross, and to the Vine Inn, Ombersley Road, and from the Cross *via* Lowesmoor to Shrub Hill. The original Tramway Trust Company was sold in 1889, and the City of Worcester Tramway Company took over the system. It went into liquidation in 1892 and was succeeded by Worcester Tramways, which operated until 1899, when British Electric Traction took over. At that time, the seven double-deck and two single-deck trams covered 1,900 miles and carried 10,000 passengers each week. In addition there were eight double-decker and three single-deck horse-'buses. Some 100 horses were used to pull the vehicles.

When Richard 'Dickie' Fairbairn became manager of the depôt in St John's in 1894, he introduced 'two-horse' vehicles but, even so, an additional third horse was necessary to climb the Bull Ring gradient. He also introduced conductors into the service. Later Dickie Fairbairn became the City's only Liberal MP.

In 1903, the Worcester Electric Tramway Company was formed and the decision was made to 'electrify' the system. All the lines had to be taken up, the gauge increased to 3' 6" and additional routes established. The upheaval took place during 1903-4 and became known as the 'Electric Tramway Siege'. Atrocious winter conditions aggravated the problem, and at times it was quite impossible to pass along City streets. Overhead power lines were installed, supported at regular intervals by posts. To supply power for the new tramway and to augment the original power plant situated at Powick Mills near Powick Bridge, a new power station was built. It was opened in Hylton Road in 1902 at a cost of £7,180. The station remained in operation until 1943.

Opening on 6 February 1904, the new electric tramway served the following routes: 1. St John's – The Cross – The Vine, Ombersley Road; 2. St Nicholas Street – Rainbow Hill (Church Road); 3. St Nicholas Street – Shrub Hill; 4. (as from 30 April 1904) The Cross – London Road (Foxwell Street); 5. (as from 2 July 1904) High Street – Bath Road (Berwick Arms); in 1906, the St John's route was extended to the Brunswick Arms in Malvern Road.

Driving an electric tram was not without hazard. Occasionally one would leave the rails, especially on the Bull Ring slope, and career into buildings. Sometimes the correct manual adjustment would fail to be made to the conducting pole between the tram and the power line when negotiating a critical junction, (for instance where the London and Bath Road routes diverged). The tram would go one way and the pole the other, bringing down the 'live' cable and damaging the pole. Steep gradients were a problem, particularly in autumn, when wet leaves clogged the track. The sand box, located next to the wheels, sprinkled sand onto the track and was most useful on these occasions.

The electric trams operated until 28 May 1928; then the six miles or so of track were ripped up in a 'mini siege' and the Midland Red Omnibus Company took over the City transport system.

ABOVE: Worcester Electric Tramway siege 1903–04: laying tram lines across Worcester Bridge in 1903, Wilesmith's timber yard in the background. (TBS/CMH) LEFT: Preparing The Cross for tram lines in 1903. (TBS/CMH) RIGHT: This is the device used to erect 'tram posts' in the City streets; posts supported wires for powering the electric trams. This is in High Street, near Elgar Brothers shop, 1903–04. (CMH)

ABOVE: The Cross c1908: Lewis Clarke's ale is being advertised at 2s 3d per dozen bottles, and to the left in the background is The Foregate and the Hopmarket area before it was completely re-built. (WC) BELOW: An electric tram at The Cross c1922 with the 'new' glass 'vestibule' windscreen fitted to protect the driver; in the background is the well-remembered Cadena Café — now neither this surprisingly shortlived 'modern' tramway system, nor the old rendez-vous remain, except as seen through the camera. (ECH)

BIBLIOGRAPHY
Principal References

Chambers, J.: *A General History of Worcester* (1820).

Green, V.: *A Survey of the City of Worcester* (1764) *The History and Antiquities of the City and Suburbs of Worcester* (1793).

Leicester, H.A.: *Forgotten Worcester* (1930) *Worcester Remembered* (1936).

Nash, T.: *Collections for the History of Worcestershire* (2 volumes, 1781).

Noake, J.: *Guide to Worcestershire* (1868) *Worcestershire Relics* (1877) *An Antiquarian Ramble through the Worcester Streets* (1888) *Worcester Nuggets* (1899).

Willis-Bund, J.W.: *The Evolution of Worcester* (1906).

Much valuable material was drawn from a selection of *Directories* of Worcester and District, published between 1855 and 1955, and from the archives of *Berrows Worcester Journal, The Evening News, Worcester Daily Echo, Worcestershire Echo* and *Worcester Daily Times*.

Additional References

General Works on Worcester History

Gwilliam, H.W.: *Old Worcester: People and Places* (volumes 1 and 2, 1977 and 1978).

Haynes, Clive and Malcolm and Adlam, Brian: *Yesterday's Town: Worcester* (1978).

Stafford, J.: *Worcester as it was* (1977).

Whitehead, D.: *The Book of Worcester* (1976).

Streets and Buildings

Beard, Douglas: *A Hundred Years in the Tything, 1877 – 1977 St Mary Magdalene* (1977).

Hughes, Pat and Molyneux, Nicholas: *Worcester Streets: Friar Street* (1984).

Hughes, Pat: *Worcester Walkabout, Cornmarket, New Street, Friar Street* (1985).

Place Names

Cameron, Kenneth: *English Place Names* (1977).

Industry and Commerce

City Museum and Art Gallery, Worcester: *Steward's Chemist Shop.*

Daily Times: Supplement: *Worcester at Work* (1903).

Fownes Brothers: *Fownes' Glove Catalogue* (1891-1892).

Fownes Brothers: *The Making of Gloves* (1906).

Frank Bryan, Ltd.: *Frank Bryan Limited, 1875-1975. 100 years of service to sport* (1975).

Hill, Evans, and Co Ltd, Worcester: *The Manufacture of Malt Vinegar* (1902).

Hull, William: *History of the Glove Trade* (1834).

Lyes, D.C.: *The Leather Glove Industry of Worcester in the Nineteenth Century* (1973).

Topham, Peter: *75 years of Co-operative Progress. A History of Worcester Co-operative Society Ltd* (1956).

Transport

City Museum and Art Gallery, Worcester: *Worcester Tramways, 1844 – 1928.*

Demaus, A.B.: *Fifty Years of the Bicycle in Worcestershire, 1880-1930* (1980).

Norris, J.E.: *The Worcester and Hereford Railway,* in the *Railway Magazine,* July, 1959 and August, 1959.

Post Office

Young, M: *A History of the Post Office of Worcester, 1685-1985* (1985).

Sports

Davis, R.J.: *Boating in Worcester in the Nineteenth Century* (1980).

Vockins, M.D.: *Worcestershire County Cricket Club. A Pictorial History* (1980).

Wartime in Worcester

Carpenter, Jeff and Owen, Brian: *Worcester at War. Aspects of Wartime Life in the City* (1985).

Grundy, Michael: *'Woodbine Willie'. Fiery Glow in the Darkness. The Life, Times and Worcester Years of the Reverend G.A. Studdert Kennedy* (1985).

INDEX

Figures in *italics* refer to illustrations

139

ENDPAPERS — FRONT: Map of the City of Worcester, 1905; BACK: Map of the City of Worcester
central area, reprinted from OS map of 1928.

SUBSCRIBERS

Presentation Copies

1 City of Worcester
2 Worcestershire & Herefordshire County Council
3 Worcester City Library
4 Michael Grundy

5 Harry & Doris Haynes
6 Malcolm Haynes
7 Clive & Gill Haynes
8 Clive & Carolyn Birch
9 Betty Wilce
10 Anna Campbell
11 R.B. Yorke & M.W. Yorke
12 Ann Moore
13 D. Hussell & Mrs C.M. Lang
14 E.D.H. Senter
15 Philip Coldicott
16 Paul Daniels
17 Mrs Muriel G. Evans
18 J.A. Wright
19 Miss D.E. Phipps
20 James Brian Adams
21 Mrs Nora Baker
22 David G. Mattick
23 Brian Draper
24 Lionel Clark
25 H.S. Field-Richards
26 Mrs B. Horne
27 Mrs V.K. Hall
28 Michael M. Wheeler
29 Marion Penfold
30 Vera M. Southam
31 Mrs Lorna J. Wilton
32 E.C. Clarke
33 R.J. Cane
34 Eric Brant
35 Ruby & Frederick Rochelle
36 Bruce & Jeanette Mercer
37 Maureen & Leslie Matthews
38 Mrs Joyce Keyes
39 Victoria & Albert Museum
40 London Guildhall Library
41 Mrs Marie Jauncey
42 Mrs Hazel Gorst
43 Grahame L. Smith
44 Mrs Margaret Tubberfield
45 P.J. Gleadall
46 R.V. Roberts
47 Alwyne & Mary James
48 Mary Ralph
49 Mrs Sheila B. Walker
50 Mrs E.M. Harris
51 H.A.G. King
52 Mary & Ken Jones
53 D.G. White
54 B.D. Southall
55 Mrs Violet Ashley
56 Alan & Pamela Bishop
57 Mrs Sheila Smart
58 Mrs D.M. Saunder
59 Derek Leavey
60 Philip Davis
61 Nicholas Tithcott

62 Brenda Tithcott
63 Rebecca S.J. Cooke
64 Judith T. Bebbington
65 Godfrey Ash
66 Mr & Mrs C.V.H. Rimell
67 Jean Hughes
68 Annette Philips
69 P.J. & M. Wellspring
70 Malcolm Young
71 D. Brook
72 Alexander McConaghy
73
74 Miss M. Holl
75 William John Payne
76 James Thomas Payne
77 Jacqueline Payne
78 Evelyn May Payne
79 Reginald Charles Bird
80 Mrs F.M. Spilsbury
81 Mrs Betty Brown
82 Mrs B.E. Sullivan
83 Marian Trow
84 Mrs V.E. Greenwood
85 Mrs W. Upcott
86 M.A. & D.R. Lewis
87 Rosemary & Mick Willmore
88 R. & J. Richardson
89 Ronald Bradrick
90 E.C. Spurr
91 Mrs Anne Bell
92 B.D.A. & M.E. Awford
93 E.C. & M.E. Awford
94 Mrs Barbara Mason
95 Mrs Elspeth M. Irwin
96 Michael Pugh
97
99 F. Beard
100 W. Mapp
101 N.R. Howell
102 J.E. Cull
103 Mrs Ivy Perkins
104 Roy Furlong
105 Mrs Lillian Gould
106 Mrs Janet Draper
107 A.L. Singleton
108 Miss Julie Moran
109 Mr & Mrs G.E. Williams
110 J.D. Kite
111 Mrs M.M. Hall
112 Glyn Cording
113 E.H. Davies
114 Raymond & Elizabeth Fowler

115 Peter J. & Penny E. Green
116 B.J. Garrett
117 E.S. Kemp
118 Diane McKenna
119 Mrs H. Tomkinson
120 George Withey
121 Margery, Robert & Christopher Davis
122 Miss Elsie Gore
123
124 D.R. Tansell
125 John & Barbara Draper
126 Canon Neil Robinson
127 Mrs E. Raybould
128 David Glover
129 C.E. Prince
130 David H. Mountford
131 Mr & Mrs G.A. Crowe
132 Sarah A. Hodge
133 Mr & Mrs Iain B. Campbell
134 Keith & Gillian Istead
135 Elizabeth Istead
136 Eileen Baylis
137 S.B. & B.J. Wild
138 Angela M. Barone
139 B.G. Wood
140 Valerie Jones
141 Ann Grunsell
142 D.G. Franklin
143 K.E. Banks
144 Mrs Gwilliam
145 H.G. May
146 William E. Randell
147 R. Sanders
148 D.A. Wynn
149 B.A. Martin
150 Monica M.N. Radburn
151 W.J. Dallow
152 Bryan E. Thompson
153 Derek A. Thompson
154 Robert F. Thompson
155 R.T. Barnes
156 Mrs Isabella Fletcher
157 Mr & Mrs G. Hill
158 Mrs Lyn Green
159 J. Tustin
160 Aileen Walker
161 L.A. Drinkwater
162 Miss Dawn Munn
163 A.W. Jas Rivers
164 J.E. Perrigo Beale
165 R.G. Clews
166 D.J. Stephens

167 Mr & Mrs Len Morris
168 Mrs P. Clarke
169 W. Gill
170 J.D. Shephard
171 Mrs Mary Bishop
172 W.H. Whitehead
173 Miss E. Bishop
174 A.E.W. Lee
175 E.A. Norman
176 H.C. Baldwin
177 C.J. Baldwin
178 Mrs K. Worthington
179 Lawrence Hughes
180 Mrs M. Norcott
181 Mrs M.R. Jones
182 Mr & Mrs K. Crump
183 A.L. Waller
184 Mrs D. Surridge
185 K.R. Ellis
186 R.V. Gormley
187 M. Drake
188 Mr & Mrs T.S. Shecraft
189 Mr & Mrs D.C. Mason
190 Mr & Mrs J. Mears
191 D.C. Andrews
192 Mrs E.D. Johnson
193 John Frederick Mutter
194 David Crawford
195 Mrs E.M. Wigley
196 Anthony G. Bethell
197 T.E. Martin
198 D.V. Pugh
199 Mr & Mrs K.J. Allen
200 Mrs M.J. Wearing
201 Mis L. Kirk
202 Mrs J. Boulter
203 J. Pinches
204 J.A. Stallard
205 B.C. Brown
206 Mrs D. Freeman
207 L. Teague
208 Mrs E.B. Hanson
209 Mrs S. Davies
210 Mrs Iris Green
211 Malcolm Simpkins
212 Colin Holmes
213 Miss Amanda J. McCully
214 B. Hope
215 Richard Hope
216 Mrs K Ballard
217 L.J. Washbrook
218 G. Daultrey
219 I.L. Bostwick
220 A.L. Watkins
221 Ian S. Chalmers
222 Mrs R. Arch
223 Mrs Beryl Everton
224 J. Trow
225 Colin Day
226 Mrs E.V. Minton
227 A.T. Minett

228 M.J. Carter	292 Mrs J.M. Racliffe	355 R. Whittaker	422 Mrs J.M. Davies
229 M.A. Rodd	293 Mrs J. Martin	356 Mrs P. Swinbourne	423 G.V. Price
230 Mrs L.M. Copson	294 Mrs J.A. Goode	357 Mrs J. Williams	424 Mrs H.J. Walters
231 R.L. Dovey	295 Ronald W.R. Clayton	358 David Smith	425 Mrs M.A. Fisk
232 G.K. Wood	296 Andrew M. Nicholls	359 R.E. Bridge	426 Mrs J.L. Richards
233 Mrs J.E. Harrison	297 R.G. Davies	360 F. Dearlove	427 Miss Sheila A. Tarran
234 Mrs M. Griffiths	298 W. Gibbs	361 D.M. Kirby	428 Betty Matthews
235 Clive Dayus	299 G. & J. Murray	362 S.J. Burton	429 K.R.B. Williams
236 Miss M.A. Clifford	300 Mrs E.L. Howson	363 D. Burton	430 Mrs M.J. Harris
237 Mrs Copson	301 Mr & Mrs J.A.	364 Michael Burnett	431 Miss G.M. Watts
238 Mr & Mrs C.J.	Willcox	365 Mrs Iris Hodgkins	432 Mrs D.M. Harman
Huckfield	302 Andrew Clark	366 Mrs S.A. Woodward	433 Miss D.N. Paine
239 Paul Amphlett	303 Mrs Christine P.	367 Mrs J.A. Anscombe	434 Eileen M. Holland
240 M.J. Blackshaw	Hawker	368 Miss M.C. Millis	435 Mrs M. Roberts
241 Mrs R. Freeman	304 J.E. Gill	369 J. & M. Ricketts	436 John & Mrs Hazel
242 Rev Gorran	305 Mrs M. Boaz	370 E. Taylor	Thorpe
Chapman	306 Mrs Maureen King	371 Richard T. Porter	437 E. Parker
243 T. Dyson	307 M.A. Howard	372 Mrs Cookson	438 W.F. & J.M. Windsor
244 B. Fennell	308 H.B.R. Penney	373 Mrs D. Turner	439 Ms J.G.M. Walden
245 Mrs Ann M.	309 Dr R.M. Peberdy	374 Mrs R. Coopey	440 Neville Knott
Nicholson	310 Miss K.L Slater	375 Mrs K. S. Sier	441 Mrs B.R. Cullis
246 H.M. Moxey	311 K. Slater	376 F.H. Lammas	442 D.H. Ball
247 G.P. Jackson	312 G. Collins	377 Mrs M. Lammas	443 Mrs V.J. Cook
248 Mrs M. Hartwright	313 Mervyn & Sonia	378 Dr R.M.H. Smith	444 Mr & Mrs P.W. Rixon
249 T.H. Dauncey	Obrey	379 Frank & Audrey	445 Mrs J. Bailey
250 A.F. Barton	314 Mrs S. Hackett	Cullis	446 S.G. Perrins
251 Mrs M. Sayers	315 Mr & Mrs D.W.	380 P.A. Shearman	447 Mrs D.M. Morris
252 H.W. Lawrence	Mountford	381 J.E. Bacon	448 F.W. Naish
253 M.J. Hebden	316 Mr & Mrs G. Burton	382 Mrs V.H. Harber	449 Mrs B. Naish
254 Miss H.F. Ladd	317 R. Webb	383 Mrs D.R. Norris	450 Mrs E.F. Hood
255 D.J. Young	318 Les & Joan Lampitt	384 Miss I. Bradley	451 Mrs D. Nash
256	319 Ray & Brenda Jones	385 Mrs W. Cocklin	452 W.G. Haines
257 T. Clapton	320 Mrs June Bennett	386 R.H. Hill	453 R.H. Gammon
258 Pamela Hurle	321 Mrs J. Baldwin	387 G.I. & S.J. Johnson	454 Mrs M. Oakey
259 D. Cottrell	322 R.T. Spink	388 D.A. & A.J. Gardner	455 Mr & Mrs P.J.S.
260 Mrs Barbara J. Wyatt	323 W.P. Paterson	389 Mr & Mrs K.C.	Willis
261 Mrs M.A. Neale	324 Mr & Mrs H.	Withers	456 S.W. Wilkins
262 Brian H. Elliot-	Huckfield	390 Mr & Mrs R.L.	457 Mrs M. Wilkinson
Williams	325 Mr & Mrs D.	Watson	458 C.R. Wilkinson
263 May, Trevor & Colin	Housman	391 Miss P.J. Rayner	459 Mrs P.E. White
Sadler	326 J.R. Lewis	392 Mrs H. Reynolds	460 G. Rose
264 F.E. Skinner	327 Miss S.D. Jones	393 Mrs S. Nash	461 A. Hodgetts
265 J.W. Nisbet	328 Mrs T.A. Morris	394 Mrs K.E. Pardoe	462 Mrs B.M. Davidson
266 Peter T. Lane	329 Mrs M.A. North	395 Peter H. Smith	463 E.G. Mutter
267 Roy Hayward	330 Mrs K. Crowe	396 R. Digger	464 M.K. Jones
268 Michael F. Oldham	331 Mrs J.E. Staples	397 Mrs E.G. Harrison	465 I.J. Rouse
269 Colin Davis	332 M. Staples	398 Ron & Betty Strain	466 J.L. Thomas
270 Peter Lloyd	333 B.J. Cope	399 G.L. Hunt	467 M.J. Power
271 Miss L.K. Wilesmith	334 D.M. Barwell	400 P.D. Inight	468 C. Kay
272 Mrs I.L. Milsom	335 Mr & Mrs W.	401 Miss E.M. Crofts	469 S.R. Knee
273 Mrs M. Armstrong	Scrivens	402 Mrs J. Crofts	470 R.J. & Mrs M.E.
274 W.J. Sudworth	336 R.A. Shuard	403 R.W. Manton	Green
275 D. Morris	337 Miss B. Shuard	404 Mrs E.L. Hine	471 D.E. Aston
276 Mrs Y.M. Kensett	338 Derrick A. Sneed	405 Mrs E.M. Clarke	472 V.J. Williams
277 J.E. Green	339 A.R. Thomas	406 Mrs Sheila B. King	473 Rev J.H. & Mrs M.E.
278 Miss B.J. Rackstraw	340 D.M. & J. Harford	407 G.H. Green	Green
279 George William Roy	341 Mrs K. Walker ✔	408 Miss E.A. Lawrence	474 B. Hackett
Palmer	342 R.J. Bunce	409 Mrs H. Stone	475 W.F. Daisley
280 N.R. Bennett	343 M. Lee	410 J.A. Probert	476 Mr & Mrs P. Smith
281 M. Averill	344 J.A. Webb	411 R.A. Cox	477 R.A. Belcher
282 D.R. Read	345 P.F. & J.M. Bridge	412 Mrs F. Long	478 Miss P. Baker
283 G. Coleman	346 Mrs J. Harrison	413 A.E. Daniels	479 Mr & Mrs W.P.
284 P. Davis	347 Mrs P. Jenkins	414 H.M. Jenkins	Mason
285 P. Wood	348 G. Dutfield	415 Patricia M. Evans	480 P.R. Stephens
286 Miss Vicky Haynes	349 Miss M.A. Palmer	416 Frank H. Brown	481 W.H. Childs
287 Alan Lewis	350 V. Clayton	417 L. Kite	482 D.M. Yapp
288 Mrs Harris	351 M. Harding	418 Mrs R.J. Lee	483 H.B. Ford
289 Mrs M. Burchell	352 G.W. Hundley	419 John F. Spiller	484 L.A. & J.M. Wood
290 F.E.A. Armes	353 L.T.J. & L.M. Cook	420 E.G. Jones	485 N.G. Price
291 Fred Orme	354 T. Downes	421 Mrs S.J. Brookes	486 John McCarthy

487 Robert Hunt	552 E.E. Farley	620 Peggy Parry	688 Mrs M. Baldwin
488 N.S. Norton	553 Mrs D.L. Willis	621 P.C. Underwood	689 S. Willis
489 Mrs Florence E. Layton	554 Miss C. Shee	622 C.E. Hill	690 L.J. Bowkett
490 Rev Owain Bell	555 Mrs B. Cottrill	623 Mrs J. Bourne	691 D. Martin
491 M.F. Bender	556 Derek Bridge	624 J.V. Luxton	692 Mrs Marjorie Davie
492 R.J. Smith	557 J.F. Bayes	625 Mrs E. McGrath	693 Edward Clissold
493 Mrs Hazel Shellam	558 Mr Lee	626 Mrs D.J. Powell	694 K.C. Tongue
494 Mr & Mrs A.C. Brookes	559 M.C. Powell	627 Mrs F.M. Smith	695 Mr & Mrs H. Brown
495 H.H. Jackson	560 S.D. Bullock	628 Mrs J. Andrews	696 A.R. Baylis
496 Mr & Mrs B.J. Tayler	561 Norman Watts	629 Mrs K.M. Hemming	697 Dr D. Brock
497 Mr & Mrs J. Evans	562 P. Nottingham	630 Mrs H. Chidlow	698 Audrey D. Tolley
498 Patrick Ailwyn Jinks	563 Mr & Mrs T.M. Shouler	631 Peter Paxford	699 Miss C.F. Moore
499 Derick Ailwyn Jinks	564 Mr & Mrs O.P. Lee	632 Mrs Doreen Babbs	700 Mrs F. Briggs
500 J.W. Dinsley	565 Mrs E.F. Shore	633 T. Nash	701 R. Birchley
501 G.B. Grandison	566 D.A. Baker	634 Mrs P.M. Jew	702 Mrs F.E. Dovey
502 W.T. Amphlett	567 Tessa Jones	635 Miss D.M. Thomas	703 Mrs B.J. Cummings
503 Miss J.E. Sprague	568 John MacLaren	636 J.M.R. Drummond	704 J. Taylor
504 M.P. Russell	569 Miss P.M. Simkin	637 L.J. Harper	705 Miss M.M. Potts
505 Mrs B.M. Bramwell	570 Brenda Roper	638 Mrs O.A. Jones	706 Alfred Shepherd
506 Nicholas J. Edwards	571 Tim Oakley	639 A. Jones	707 Miss D. Milward
507 Stanley W. Smith	572 Rev P.J. Leverton	640 David & Agnes Young	708 Mrs J. Berry
508 George Lewis	573 Mrs Glenda Wilce	641 P.J. Hodgkiss	709 A.J. Hughes
509 C. Hughes	574 G.F. Jordan	642 Mrs N. Hall-Dixon	710 Miss H.A. Jones
510 Mrs M.E. Morse	575 W.J. Griffiths	643 Mrs N.D. Constant	711 Mrs P.M. Lloyd
511 Mrs A. Turner	576 R.J. Dean	644 G.M. Beard	712 G. Nairn
512 Peter J. Kimberley	577 K.W. Baker	645 F.C.H. Dayus	713 David Rastall
513 J.R. & O.L. Thoumine	578 A.D. White	646 Mrs C. Young	714 Mrs J. Griffiths
514 R.A. Hartland	579 Mrs K. Sheppard	647 Edna Mann	715 Mrs P. Law
515 A.J. Cook	580 Mrs Joan M. Parsons	648 Mrs G. Darling	716 Mrs B. Buckman
516 C.L. Gallagher	581 Barbara E. Morley	649 Mrs P. Clarke	717 Mr & Mrs T.J. Kendrick
517 Angela & Cyrus Baria	582 Megan Wooler	650 Miss V. Tedham	718 Mr & Mrs Chafer
518 Wendy A. Townsend	583 Dorothy Lunt	651 Mrs M. Woodfine	719 H.H. Grundy
519 Stefan Jarkowski	584 J.W.J. Hudson	652 Mrs A. Hobkirk	720 Mr & Mrs H.W. Banks
520 Mrs Margaret Lloyd-James	585 Dennis Evans	653 Mrs L.M. Andrews	721 Miss Mary Jack
521 Mrs D.E. Estell	586 Mrs Gloria Chapman	654 Mrs D.J. Jarkowska	722 Len Sherriff
522 Phillip & Helen Curtis	587 Trevor Watkins	655 Miss M.E. Reynolds	723 Mrs Bromwyn Wells
523 John Hadley	588 R.C. Smith	656 A.M. Bullock	724 Les Beswick
524 Mrs D. Jinks	589 Mr & Mrs B.J. Pingriff	657 Mrs J. Hemming	725 Mrs C.M. Harris
525 Mrs Avis Owen	590 R.K. Young	658 Mrs S. Banfield	726 Marguerite Stevens
526 N.J. Mills	591 Mrs E.A. Myatt	659 Mrs B.J. Price	727 R.G. Fidoe
527 Mrs T. Horsley & E. Hanley	592 Margaret Lowe	660 P. Bowen	728 I.N. Bramich
528 Mrs J. Blake	593 Miss W.S. Hope	661	729 Valerie Steed
529 C. Thomas	594 Nick Fowler	662 Canon W.J. Reynolds	730 Douglas Story
530 Michael Boswell	595 Mrs Valerie S. Brown	663 Miss Deborah Ann Taylor	731 T.J. Bridges
531 Granham Cox	596	664 Mrs Pat Hopkins	732 Mrs L. Hawkins
532 Royston Thomas Slim	598 A.G. Luscombe	665 Mr & Mrs T. Maybury	733 John Bowkett
533 Janus Books	599 Eric Giles	666 T.J. Hall	734 Gemma Louise Schoolcraft
534 H.V.J. Fowler	600 Miss N.W. Hughes	667 Mrs A.J. Haywood	735 R.C. Knight
535 I. Hughes	601 Mrs Linda George	668 Ms D. Bufton	736 Mr & Mrs W.P. Dovey
536 P.S. Inight	602 Mrs J. Gilbert	669 Mrs J.L. Russell	737
537 Mrs J. Morris	603 Mrs G. Lawrence-Smith	670 Ian & Stuart Stock	738 Alice Hughes
538 Dr A.G. Fielding	604 Mrs King	671 E.W. Avery	739 J.S. Williams
539 L. Morris	605 Mrs E. Brooks	672 Mrs E.M. Jones	740 Miss Wade
540 L. Simpson	606 F.W. Thomasson	673 Mrs S.B. Smith	741 P.J. Daniel
541 Mrs C.M. Evans	607 T.J. Green	674 Miss A.E. Jenkins	742 B. Purvis
542 J. Willis	608 Mrs B. McLean	675 R.R. Morris	743 Barbara Pearson
543 M.T. Strain	609 R.W. Simmonds	676 Mrs Ruth Porter	744 Mrs C.A. Stanley
544 Mrs Witcombe	610 Pat McCulway	677 C.F. Owens	745 L.S. Bradley
545 Mrs M. Owens	611 K. Allsop	678 P.A. Ellis	746 J.C. Bishop
546 Mrs M.D. Wakefield	612 Mrs S. Norris	679 Miss F.B.R. Probert	747 Miss E.R. Ellis
547 Mrs D. Wigby	613 T.F. Wilmore	680 Mr & Mrs M.J. Blundell	748 Mrs H.D. Clifton
548 Alan Bishop	614 D. Barnett	681 F. Barrow	749 R.E. Gummery
549 Mrs G. Rata	615 Miss Janet Baker	682 P.J. Gordon	750 A.M. Whortley
550 R. Hines	616 Mrs P.A. Morgan	683 Miss M. Joy Hatton	751 Canon Romilly Craze
551 Mrs P.A. Salter	617 Mrs I. Jones	684 M. Hope	752 Andrew Craze
	618 Mrs L.A. Pratt	685 N.E. Dilks	753 Rosalind Stanley
	619 Gordon Knight	686 Elizabeth Long	754 Leon James Barton
		687 T.F. Turner	755 Mrs J.K. MacTaggart

756 Mrs E. Sampson
757 W.G. Jones
758 Mrs A. Penney
759 R.J. Young
760 Brian Reginald Chadd
761 Melanie J. Hewins
762 Norman Brown
763 D.O. Shuker
764 P.H.M. Lunn
765 R.G. Nunney
766 Stuart Harvey Griffiths
767 Mrs Peggy Lumsden
768 Mrs W. Cocklin
769 W.F.J. Blueman
770 C. Allsopp
771 Mr & Mrs R. Dorricott
772 Mrs A. Brown
773 Mrs J.N. Bishop
774 Mrs M.E. Taylor
775 Mrs J. Fry
776 Mrs A. Busby
777 Edward & Ruth Reeves
778 Mrs B.R. Cullis
779 Ian R. Brace
780 P. Scoggins
781 Mrs M.J. Badham
782 V.T. Gwilliam
783 J.F. Harrison
784 John C. Brace
785 Eileen Haines
786 D. Gwilliam
787 C.W. Voyce
788 Mr & Mrs S. Winstone
789 Mr & Mrs H. Fewson
790 Mrs C. Meiklejohn
791 Joan L. Smith
792 Patricia J. Smith
793 John H. Mulgrew
794 Joe Walter
795 Mrs Maureen J. Grant
796 Mrs A. Gray
797 Nigel Bullock
798 Hilary Fisher
799 Miss F.E. White
800 D.C. Smallman
801 A.T. Davis
802 Mrs D.U. Freeman
803 Mrs J. Patton
804 Vincent Durkin
805 R.A. Phillips
806 Mr & Mrs E. Chauncer
807 J.J. Roberts
808 A.T. Marshall
809 Mrs J. Malby
810 G.W. Harris
811 Mrs J.A. Samuels
812 Mrs Celia Gardner
813 John Purser
814 R.A. Fisher ✓
815 D.J. Walker ✓
816 Alan S. Adamson
817 D.R. Skinner
818 Mrs W.A. Gore
819 Mrs P.J. Barrett
820 M.H. Box
821 Mrs D. Cooper

822 J.L. Thomas
823 L.J. Morris
824 Margaret Butler
825 D.L. Stevens
826 Geoffrey Aston
827 C.R. Hindley
828 Mrs S. Dawson
829 S.D. Coad
830 John Mann
831 L.W. Bayes
832 N.R. Jones
833 J.P. Richards
834 Mrs Eileen Lawrence
835 Mrs M. Ovington
836 Charles F. Hodges MBE
837 J.C. Mulligan
838 Richard William Nokes
839 A.P. Peters
840 D. Edwards
841 Mr & Mrs T. Haskoll
842 B.R. Slater
843 Mrs F. Hound
844 Mr & Mrs Nigel Woodhouse
845 Mrs Y. Clutterbuck
846 N.P. Forster
847 A.F. Grayson
848 D.W. Newman
849 B. Coppin
850 R.M. Darke
851 A.W. Merrell
852 Mrs Diane Healey
853 M.B. Powell
854 J.A. Shaw
855 P. Porteus
856 Mrs D. Inskip
857 Mrs Matthews
858 Mrs D. Morris
859 Miss B.M. Beer
860 Mrs Biffen
861 Mrs M. Plant
862 Mrs J.A. Wood
863 J.B. Wadey
864 Mrs V. Richards
865 John Corbett
866 Tim Good
867 Miss J. Griffiths
868 Mrs J.A. Ager
869 Mrs E. A Howes
870 J. Marshall
871 Mrs J. Penlington
872 Mrs Milton-Willnott
873 R. Gregory
874 David J. Davies
875 P.W. Grinnell
876 D.J. Trigg
877 K.A. Roberts
878 C. Gittins
879 George H. Davies
880 F.E.C. Beech
881 N.W. Carver
882 Caroline Harmes
883 Mrs M. Owen
884 R.W. Spencer
885 Miss A.E. Griffiths
886 Mrs B. Churchill
887 R. Reece
888 Mrs T. Weston

889 R.G. Murray
890 R. Reece
891 Mrs P. Fryer
892 G.R. Ruff
893 Gwen Morris
894 Winifred M. Evans
895 Idris J. Norman
896 Edward Bedford
897 A.T. Shearman
898 Paul G. Yunnie
899 J. Bullock
900 Martin John Allen
901 Margaret Williams
902 Ron & Heather Burse
903 R.W. Smith
904 Martin Chapple
905
908 George H. Nash
909 Gilbert J. Griffiths
910 Mr & Mrs Merrell
911 Lucy Valerie Harvey
912 Gordon Jones
913 Jeremy Price
914 Mr & Mrs A.E. Banner
915 Cora Weaver
916 A.B. Merrett
917
918 C.E. Grant
919 Brian M. O'Brien
920 L.J. Bushell
921 Peggy Pringle
922 Michael Carter
923 E.N. Heywood
924 Mr & Mrs A.J. Wood
925 C.A. & A.J. Wood
926 Mr Cordles
927 Geoffrey Holroyde
928 Mrs Dorothy A. Pace
929 R.C. Lovegrove
930 Mrs D. Hope
931 John Charles James
932 Mrs Dorothy James
933 Mrs Joan E. Hanson
934 Mrs F. Drake
935 Robert John Price
936 E.D. Rayers
937 Pamela Saunders
938 D.W.R. Dixon
939 Julia A. Tuckey
940 Christopher J. Tuckey
941 George Cook
942 Mrs E. Watkins
943 George F. Badham
944 Jean M. Turner
945 Denise Lee Curtis
946 Johann Louise Curtis
947
948 Mrs M.C. Hayes
949 Mrs J.M. Sandford
950 Stella Round
951 Michael J. Hawkins
952 R.J. Matthews
953 G.H. Prosser
954 Graheme Stuart Barson
955 Helen D. Barson
956 Mrs Daphne Hill
957 Jenny Breeze
958 A.W. Wright

959 J.R. Hamlett
960 John Talbot Cooper
961 Colin E. Mountford
962 B.D. O'Halloran
963 Jeanette Moores
964 Marjorie Lock
965 R.H. & J. Osborne
966 Christine & Roger Russell
967 D. Collins
968 Cyril James Howell
969 Alfred Edward Taylor
970 David Andrew Taylor
971 Beryl B. Sandland
972 D. Rowberry
973 B. Price
974 Mrs Z. O'Hara
975 Angela Mary Woodhall
976 A.J. Checketts
977 J.D. Cornes
978 F.T. Lannie
979 Frank W. Beach
980 Jean K. King
981 Miss Kathleen M. Veare
982 Mrs Peggy Waldwyn
983 Worcester Sixth Form College
984 Mrs F. Hollis
985 Miss M. Hooper
986 John Maylett
987 Austin Russell Pugh
988 J.M. Mulligan
989 R.R. Tearne
990 A.T. Oliver
991 Gordon Philip Griffiths
992 F. & F. Troth
993 A.J. Winwood
994 Mrs V.U. Mueller
995 Robert Rayers
996 John Rayers
997 Mr & Mrs D.B. Cox
998 Richard Darling
999 Mrs & Mrs Charles S. Pigg
1000 Mrs P. Lloyd
1001 Hereford &
1036 Worcester Libraries Department
1037 N.J. Hinton
1038 Mrs B.M. Parker
1039 Eva Powell
1040 E. Roger Thomas
1041 A.J. Hayes
1042 Derek Jones
1043
1044 Ronald Claud Cook
1045 Stephen Lloyd
1046 C.R. Thompson
1047 G.E. Green
1048 E.H. Sargeant
1049 Bertram W. Walters
1050 V.J. Brigginshaw
1051 I.R. Edwards
1052 I.R.O. Brettell
1053 W.P. Briggs
1054 R.O. Kirkby
1055 Frederick William Edward Pugh

1056 P.A. Bodily	1125 Mr & Mrs W.H. King	1187 T.C. Farmbrough	1249 Mrs Janet W. Probert
1057 L.W. Haughtey	1126 Mrs R.A. Evans	1188 Margaret Tarran	1250 G.R. Fletcher
1058 J.W. Brazier	1127	1189 Mrs R.M. Cottrill	1251 Bernard Owen
1059 Mrs M.E. Aston	1128 William Arthur	1190 William John Davies	1252 K.C. Blackwell
1060 S. Waddington	Burgess	1191 Miss Ann Stallard	1253 John Corbett
1061 H.W. Hencher	1129 C.E. Poole	1192 Major G.D.K.	1254 Patricia Richards
1062 M. Jones	1130 Mrs Margaret Bartlett	Woolrych MBE	1255 John Marshall
1063 Kevin Clarke	1131 H. Griffin	1193 C.D. Collings	1256 Mrs M.J. Schmidl
1064 J.D. Langford	1132 Geoffrey King	1194 Rev D. Beard	1257 D.G. Barrett
1065 Robin E.J. Chater	1133 John & Margaret	1195 Eric & Jane	1258 Emma Brown
1066 John Nevlle Chater	Bradley	Waterhouse	1259 T. Taylor
1067 Mrs N. McGorrigaw	1134 J.M. & P.J. Brazier	1196 D.F. Bench	1260 K.B. Price
1068 Mrs Brenda Joan	1135 Mrs T.D. Spencer	1197 Colin Hughes	1261 A.J. Shergold
Conway	1136 Desmond Symonds	1198 Mrs E.M. Preece	1262 Mrs B.W. Williams
1069 E.J. Pardoe	1137 Dennis Ogle	1199 City of Worcester –	1263 Douglas Laird
1070 Muriel Richardson	1138 Dr & Mrs B.S. Bennett	City Architect &	1264 Rosalind Boynton
1071 Mrs Stella M. Cronin	1139 Mrs P.A. Wilson	Planning Officers'	1265 Ruby Kloock
1072 Simon Cronin	1140 D. & K.R. Edynbry	Department	1266 Miss Susan Bujanszki
1073 Irene Smallman	1141 Howard Davis	1200 Mrs Joyce Wright	1267 Mrs Ann Bujanszki
1074 Audrey Smith	1142 L. Cox	1201 Anthony G. Hail	1268 J.T. Haines
1075 Richard Trevor East	1143 Mrs M. Freebee	1202 Paula Shaw	1269 C. Whitehouse
1076 Alice M. Williams	1144 Margaret I. Hardwick	1203 Mrs B. Ridings	1270 John Brooker
1077 Beryl C.F. Hughes	1145 Stuart M. Bee	1204 Mrs D. Perry	1271 George Crowley
1078 Mr & Mrs G. Podmore	1146 Marcel Callow	1205 Mrs J. Fenwick	1272 Andrew Lock
1079 A.M. & J.M. White	1147 Mrs Sheila Suthard	1206 Edward Reeves	1273 Susan Greenshill
1080 J.H. Wells	1148 N.R. Goode	1207 Ruth Reeves	1274 Brian Roberts
1081 John Bonnett	1149 Frank Huxley	1208	1275 Eileen Fowler
1082 A.J.W. Gill	1150 John Alan Wilkes	1209 Kenneth Alan Lander	1276 Christopher Pancheri
1083 F. Breakwell	1151 D. Crook	1210 Michael Peach	1277 Nellie Wood
1084 L.E. Hall	1152 J.E.G. Evans	1211 Lt Cdr A.G. Thomas	1278 Mrs M. Wallace
1085 Steve Moore	1153 Ray & Kathleen	RN	1279 P.C. Scaiff
1086 Mrs P.M. Cullis	Lawrence-Smith	1212 Hazel R. Simon	1280 S.F. Hedworth
1087 Raymond Powell	1154 Stuart Lane	1213 Mrs Cynthia Harding	1281 Gerald I. Haynes
1088 D.E. Dunand	1155 Worcester City	1214 Mrs Doreen Pugh	1282 Terence Wells
1089 Miss P.A.G. Burrows	Museum	1215 John L. Potter	1283 Marjorie Bullock
1090 J.H. Cave	1156	1216 R.C. Howse	1284 J.C. Sparkes
1091 A.K. Saunders	1157 T.G.A. Baker	1217 John Merrick	1285 Coleen Mary
1092 T.L. & A.H. Nickson	1158 Suzanne Eglesfield	1218	Bickerton
1093 Mrs A. Jenkins	1159 L.W. Pace	1219 R.A. Wiltshire	1286 Katie & Alex
1094 Alan C. Wood	1160 Mrs E. Allen	1220 John Worthington	Bickerton
1095 C.J. Morrall	1161 Beryl & Ivor Raundle	1221 Kathleen	1287 N.H. Parker
1096 Mrs Ann Bradley	1162 R. Lampitt	Worthington	1288 Miss M. Tredwell
1097 Owain & Kim Bell	1163 Mrs P.L. Taylor	1222	1289 Olive M. Jenkins
1098 Mavis Ridley	1164 Colin & Jacqueline	1223 H. Cooling	1290
1099 R.S. Wheeler	Hartwright	1224 Richard Larkham	1292 Mrs B. Hewlett
1100 Mrs J. Dow	1165 Margery J. Smith	1225 Roger C. Waters	1293 Andrew Jenkinson
1101 Mrs Barbara Good	1166 Mrs B. Stroker	1226 Mrs B.M. Aston	1294 A.C. Skinner
1102 Marin Chase ✓	1167 P.J. Stroker	1227 Mrs A.E. Ross-Caton	1295 K. Knowles
1103 Marie & Dennis Large	1168 T.S. Crosby	1228 D.W. Fryer	1296 R.W. Merry
1104 Joan Spooner	1169 Pamela M. Sandford	1229 Mrs Beryl J. Holmes	1297 D.S. Vernall
1105 John & Kate Hooper	1170 S.W. & G.R. Finch	1230 Alan & Megan Hayes	1298 Adam Bench
1106 Mrs P.D. Woodman	1171 Mrs E.I. Harrison	1231 David & Debbie Cox	1299 R. Oliver
1107 Mr & Mrs J.A. Glover	1172 Kenneth C. Martin	1232 Tony & Mary Hadley	1300 Jennifer Read
1108 B. Pedlingham	1173 W.T. Cook, S.J. Cook	1233 Ivor & Brenda Cox	1301 Sandy & Geoff Coates
1109 Anthony M. Jenkins	& M. Carnall	1234 G.L. Redgrave	1302 Dinah Ann Verman
1110 A.J. Westcott	1174 G.A. & L.D.W. Lycett	1235 David Burbidge	1303 Lt-Cdr A.G. Thomas
1111 Hilary Jakeman	1175 P.J. & P.E. Maylor	1236 Kenneth G. Price	RN
1112 Norton T. Thatcher	1176 Mrs S.M. Thomas	1237 Maurice H. Price	1304 Dinah Ann Verman
1113	1177 Anna M. Worsley	1238 Margaret A. White	1305 Michael Peach
1114 Tony Chapman	1178 Doris & Jack	1239 Hilda A. Price	1306 M.E. Denham
1115 William Edwin Jones	Stephens	1240 A. & S.C. Thompson	1307 Mrs Hazel Warner
1116 Christine Jones	1179 Sylvia Gascoyne	1241 Mrs E.W. Shergold	1308 Eileen Jean Watson
1117 Ken & Jean Jones	1180 David & Jennifer	1242 K.G. Clarke	1309 John Alexander
1118 Michael Ford	Gascoyne	1243 Roy Jauncey	1310 R.M. Sinclair
1119 Josephine Wilson	1181 Rodney Gascoyne	1244 Mrs Joan Gould	1311 Derrick & Margaret
1120	1182 C.D. Jones	1245 Brian John Harris	Watson
1121 Jean P. Howels	1183 John Hemingway	1246 Miss Hazel Amy	1312 R.B. Lockett
1122 Mrs D.R. Fenn	1184 J. Raymon Lewis	Birch	1313 Mrs J. Graham
1123 Alfred Merrell	1185 John A. Yelland	1247 Mr & Mrs J. Kerrigan	1314 Mrs A.B. Miller
1124 C.G. Cale	1186 J.R. Edwards	1248 Miss E.V. Allen	1315 Jas Carr

1316 J.S. Phillips-Broadhurst	1382 John Colin Austin	1449 A.R. & V. Griggs	1514 Jean Brown
1317	1383 R. Sayers	1450 Brian Collett	1515 B.M. Hebden
1319 Mrs M. Rimell	1384 Mr & Mrs J.C. Lampitt	1451 Mrs Ivy D. Smith	1516 B.P. Milton
1320 Donald Hunt	1385 A. Bryan	1452 R.A. Blandford	1517 J.R.E. Browne
1321 J.J. Roberts	1386 B.F. Savage	1453 Joan Hinks	1518 Arthur William Fewtrell
1322 Mrs M. Wainwright	1387 Alfred F. Wilkes MBE	1454 Brent Downey	1519 J. Forrest Penman
1323 Edith F. Cochett	1388 Mrs M.M. Stinton	1455 M.D. Rosewarne	1520 Ruth Boyd
1324 Beryle McIlmurray	1389 Sidney Partridge	1456 Mrs Janet Morrell	1521 Robin Steel
1325 D.R. Jefferies	1390 Mr & Mrs W. Fereday	1457 Mr & Mrs Paul Daniels	1522 Mrs B.J. Owen
1326 Christine Wyard	1391 D.D. Carleton	1458 Mr & Mrs J. Raisen	1523 T.M.A. Campbell
1327 Miss M.E. Compton	1392 Mrs A.L. Penney	1459 Miss Paula Mitchell	1524 David Turner
1328 Mrs K. Brannen	1393	1460 Mrs F.A. Wagstaff	1525 H.L.W. Hope
1329 N.J. Hunting	1396 Anthony G. Bethell	1461 Mrs S.E. Finbow	1526 Raymond Monk
1330 J.T. Chase	1397 Colin Anthony Day	1462 Mrs Pat Simmons	1527 Rev O.J.T. Roberts MA
1331 J.R. Martin	1398 Philip Hytch	1463 Mrs Jean Kimpton	1528 John Matthews
1332 Jessie Elte	1399 Mrs M.M. Westwood	1464 Georgina Firth	1529 M.J. Tranter
1333 Helen Pollard	1400 Miss F.E. White	1465 Lynett Vernall	1530
1334 D.C. Summerfield	1401 H. Hodges	1466 Mrs Heather Stone	1531 Mrs E. Staley
1335 J.S. Pickford	1402 Rev J.M. & Mrs Marsh	1467 Mrs Susan Nash	1532 Steven & Michelle Price
1336 Mrs M. Hayton	1403 G.W. & M.J. Mann	1468 Miss G.M. Oldfield	1533 Jean Mary Chidlow
1337 Maureen Butcher	1404 Mr & Mrs William L. Lee	1469 W.A. & J.A. Carey	1534 Roger Massey
1338 Marjorie B. Wright	1405 Eric Lathem	1470 Janet Ford	1535 Cheryl Jensen
1339 John Fawkes	1406 Dorothy Edwards	1471 Mary Mann	1536 Dr Eurfyl Richards
1340 N.G. Drury	1407 P.B. Richardson	1472 Mrs Jane Bodimeade	1537 D.J. Browning
1341 Miss Mabel Joyce Cox	1408 Irene Roberts	1473 Mrs Marilyn Lewis	1538 .G. Fairbairn
1342 Mrs Lilian R. Hooker	1409 H.T. Steade	1474 Mr & Mrs S.P. Evison	1539 Anne Evans
1343	1410 Trevor J. Staite	1475 John Martin Lester	1540 Peter W. Coleman
1344 L.M.S. Blythman	1411 Geoffrey Thompson	1476 Mrs Peggy G. Rudd	1541 Kathleen Ramsey
1345 Lynne Turberfield	1412 Donald D. Cox	1477 Peter Harber	1542 Doreen May Babbs
1346 J. Barton	1413 Arnold Bryan	1478 Mr & Mrs Barry Guise	1543 Dr H.P. Phillips
1347 Rt Hon Peter Walker MBE MP	1414 E.J. Rivers	1479 Mrs B.A. Plant	1544 W.M. Brown
1348 Mr & Mrs M.R. Potter	1415 Edward Moule	1480 Agnes Sheward	1545 Marion Simmons
1349 Miss I. Allen	1416 P.G. Dorrell	1481 Miss Anthea Fuller	1546 Leicester University Library
1350 Mrs Jane Broomfield	1417 Mrs Joyce Harding	1482 Mrs L.A.E. Duke	1547 F. Allsopp
1351 Raida Kassim	1418 D. Higley	1483 Edwin L. Howell	1518 Mr & Mrs A.H.G. Blocksidge
1352 W.E. Smith	1419 Denis Howells	1484 W.O. Fielding	1549 The Kings School, Worcester
1353 Mrs Bella Holt	1420 Mr & Mrs E.L. Clifton-Crick	1485 Mrs R.M. Harber	1550 V.M. Hoyle
1354 Mrs W. Cleverly	1421 G.R. Brunyee	1486 Robert Smith	1551 V. & M. Bunn
1355 R.D. Weaver	1422 K.J. Clifford	1487 Mrs V.M. Mooney	1552 Sylvia Ann Hayes
1356 Mr & Mrs A.E. Stallard	1423 Brian R. Chadd	1488 Mrs P.M.A. Farquharson	1553 Geoffrey James Taylor
1357	1424	1489 S. Williams	1554 Joan Catherine Matty
1358 Mrs A.D. West	1426 Mrs M. Richardson	1490 Raymond Worthington	1555 Dr H.P. Phillips
1359 A.L. Edwards	1427 L.W. Park	1491 Richard Worthington	1556 C.G.D. Smith
1360 O. Griffiths	1428 G.M. Burden	1492 Garry Worthington	1557 A.M. Wherry
1361 C.E. Clarke	1429 Angela R. White	1493 J.M. Stanley	1558 Peter C. Prosser
1362 J.T. Dinley	1430 T.E. Allcott	1494 Miss S. Underhill	1559 Peter Merry
1363 G.O. Wood	1431 R.G. Murray	1495 Graham James Hooper	1560 A.H. Knight
1364 Mrs M. Carey	1432 M.B. Tetley	1496 Mrs P.A. White	1561 Miss L.M. Roberts
1365 Mrs F.M. Napper	1433 Richard C.H. Fairbairn	1497 Alison Ricketts	1562 J.F. Gittins
1366 M.H. Young	1434 Mrs Mary Billingham	1498 Bart Ricketts	1563 Charles Clemens
1367 Mrs A.M. Pearson	1435 E.A. Foskett	1499 Mrs Dorothy Insall	1564 Hereford & Worcester County Museum
1368 Mark & Jane Saunders	1436 G. Phelps	1500 Mrs Joan M. Owens	
1369 Mrs M.M. Sharp	1437 Kenneth Harrison	1501 John Horwood	1565 Ivan M. Bellamy
1370 G.D. Pickering	1438 Deborah Ryland	1502 Matthew William Griffiths	1566 Mrs K. Andrews
1371 Anthony David Cooper	1439 Michael & Carol Hallett	1503 Steve Ashton	1567 William A. Ratcliff
1372 Mrs Jessie Garlick	1440 Yardley Scully	1504 P.W. Taylor	1568 Mrs S. Bright
1373 E. Emsen	1441 Glenn Perkins	1505 R. Allkins	1569 R.H. Glover
1374 Stanley G. Harris	1442 Ray & Annette Hume	1506 David N. Warner	1570 M. Storey
1375 D.J.B. Tait	1443 Mrs P. Cook	1507 J. Pithouse	1571 Dr Marshall Wilson
1376 P. Clifford & K.J. Clifford	1444 T.K. Sharp	1508 Mrs B.N.C. Collier	1572 C.A. Tunstall
1377 Joan Sanders	1445 Dorothy Northam	1509 Mrs P. Raven	1573 Dave & Caole Pingriff
1378 Gerald Brunyee	1446 Worcester Art Furnishings	1510 Glenn A. Barker	1574 Mrs R. Ruff
1379 Margaret A. Norton	1447 P. Birkbeck	1511 John F. Wood	
1380 C. Pingriff	1448 Gordon Carter	1512 T.W. Badgery	
1381 Ray & Val Hodgkinson		1513 M.W. Brown	

1575 Michael A. Bendall	1632 D. Thomas	1696 Mrs S. Law	1754 Mrs B. Sykes
1576 Tony Yorke Brookes	1633 C.E. Wilkes	1697 D.K. Williams	1755
1577 Cherry Orchard	1634 J.E. Parker	1698 J. Cooper	1756 R.O. Walker
Primary School,	1635 Mrs Stretch	1699	1757 Mrs Kay Ballard
Worcester	1636 Mrs S. Whitehouse	1700 J.R. Boyce	1758
1578 W.J.D. Malsbury	1637 Mrs E. I. Saunders	1701	1759 Miss C.V. Powick
1579 Philip David Nunn	1638 J. Samwell	1702 Miss E.A. Cadbury	1760 Mr & Mrs N.L.
1580 M.J. Heath	1639 Miss L. Turberfield	1703	Hodgetts
1581 N.S. Gardner	1640 Mrs A. Preece	1704 R. Birkett	1761 D.E.J. Powick
1582 Mrs D. Williams	1641 Mrs S. Valentine	1705 Mrs M. Jackson	1762 Lt Col D.R. Hildick-
1583 Mrs J. Shirvington	1642 MRs M. Gwynne	1706 John & Caroline	Smith
1584 C.W. Holder	1643 A.W.H. Gordon	Roslington	1763 Mr & Mrs W. Rees
1585 John & Mavis	1644 A.J. Chilton	1707 Sue Rolt	1764 Mrs P.M. Clarke
Ricketts	1645 Mrs M.B. Thompson	1708 Mr & Mrs J. Smith	1765 N.H. Hills
1586 Mark J. Ricketts	1646 R.W. Summers	1709 Jeffery Robert	1766 P.J. Hamilton-
1587 Neil D. Ricketts	1647 D.A. Homer	Fenwick	Herbert
1588 Miss Sharon J.	1648 Mrs I. Beck	1710 Mrs J.R. Tyler	1767 David G. Dance
Ricketts	1649 D.A. Homer	1711 Mrs I.O. Austen	1768 Stuart Hamilton-Dick
1589 Colin & Trixie Glover	1650 Mrs S. Barnett	1712 Mrs Jean Ingram	1769 Gary & Sue Beaudro
1590 Clive Simpkins	1651 Mrs D.M. Wilding	1713 Janette D. Birbeck	1770 R.J. Dommett
1591 P. Thackeray	1652 T. Mann	1714 Maureen Ann Draper	1771 D. Walker
1592 Reginald P. Bryan	1653 P.A. Riley	1715 Geoffrey Webb	1772 John Steele
1593 R.E. James-	1654 T.J. Harriss	1716	1773 Mark Steele
Robertson	1655 Mrs M.E. Smith	1717 Mrs A.W.J. Johnson	1774 Mrs H. Cooper
1594 Mr & Mrs Hugh	1656 T.R. Hill	1718	1775 Mrs P.E. Cooper
Wotherspoon	1657 C.J. Clarke	1719 Dss Ruth Wintle	1776 Mr & Mrs R.D.
1595 Clive & Gill Haynes	1658 Mrs L. Bosley	1720 Mrs C.L. Lane	Yarnold
1596 Malcolm L.D. Haynes	1659 F.W.K. Spratley	1721 The Ven F.W.H.	1777 Mrs Christine
1597 Peter Hartley	1660 D.H. Bevan	Bentley	Sheppard
1598 Ann Hartley	1661 J.G. Andrews	1722 Mrs Jane Wheeler	1778 Mrs Diane
1599 M.V. Bladen	1662 R.B. Houghton	1723 R.S. Thompson	Whitehouse
1600 V.G. Parker	1663 Helen Libby	1724 D. Anderson	1779 Lindsay Smith
1601 R. Amphlett	1664 J.R.E. Moreton	1725 E.W. Bonnett	1780 Geoffrey John Jinks
1602 G.D. Garbett	1665 Mrs M. Owen	1726 Mrs F.R. Short	1781 Mr & Mrs T.J. Warner
1603 Lorna Archer	1666 Mrs J. McAnoy	1727 B.E. Richards	1782 J.D. & Mrs J.D. Harris
1604 B. Kelly	1667 G.C. Wyatt	1728 Owen Nankivell	1783 Mrs Margaret
1605 D.R. Banks	1668 M.B. Thomas	1729 Eileen Turner	Ballinger
1606 John Devereux	1669 Mrs D. Baggott	1730 John Reynolds	1784 J.J. Taylor
1607 Jeremy Vernon	1670 R.A. Lord	1731 J.G. Cambridge	1785 Mrs A. House
Carvill	1671 Mrs Dorothy Plant	1732 Canon J.O.C.	1786 G.R. Warman
1608 Mrs M.E. Bromage	1672 Mrs J. Hargreaves	Champion	1787 Trevor Martin Vale
1609 Mr Digger	1673 Mrs W. Evans	1733 S.H.R. Brown	1788 R.M. & Mrs Fisher
1610 Elizabeth Raine	1674	1734 Mrs A.G. Dyer	1789 Michael Kenneth
1611 E.M.J. Porter	1675 Mrs McManus	1735 Mrs A.V. Tarbuck	Rastall
1612 Michael Heath	1676 Mr & Mrs H. Stone	1736	1790 Leonard Thomas
1613 Geraldine Meers	1677 Mrs H.R. Mann	1737 G.B. Noble	Morris
1614 M.G. Willmott	1678 Mrs Massey	1738 Nancy Bennett	1791 Andrew Colin Taylor
1615 B.D. Kelly	1679 R.J. Sandel	1739 M. MacDonald	1792 Mrs Edith John
1616 Mrs C. Syles	1680 Ann Bentley	1740 B.M. Bates	Withey
1617 Mrs D. Glabone	1681 Julian Pugh	1741 G.W. & M.H. Fynn	1793 Miss Rene Evans
1618 Maureen Draper	1682 Mrs E. Margetts	1742 Mrs Vera Heggie	1794 Mrs Peggy Price
1619 Mrs S.A. Whitehouse	1683 Mrs M. Robinson	1743 Mrs Francis Virr	1795 Mrs G. Garland
1620 N.W. Hawker	1684	1744 Mrs J.D.M. Smith	1796 David Brookes
1621 David H.S. Ellis	1685 K.W. Ridley-Jones	1745 Mrs A. Elt	1797 D. Baggot
1622 Suzanne L.J. Ellis	1686 Mrs K. Price	1746 Mrs Pauline Bedhall	1798 R. Morris
1623 Mrs M. Woodyatt	1687 Mrs F. Calcott	1747 Mrs B. Stockhall	1799 Hilary Nicholls
1624 Mrs W. Bloodworth	1688 G.T. Fryer	1748	1800 Mr & Mrs R.E.
1625 II.J. Coleman Mrs	1689 Mrs M. Hughes	1749 Anthony John	Widdowson
1626 T.B. Duckworth	1690 K.T. Wright	Nicholls	1801 A.D. McGuirk
1627 Mrs Jennifer Evans	1691 Mrs Yvonne Bennett	1750 Mrs B. Stott	
1628 John G. Ranford	1692 P. White	1751 Mrs M. Wall	
1629 N.E. Dilks	1693 R.J. Holloway	1752 J.C. Worthington	
1630 J. Hancocks	1694 W.E. Smith	1753 Douglas & Christine	
1631 Mrs. S. Taylor	1695 Mrs R. Fortey	Dring	*Remaining names unlisted*